180 Faith-Charged Games

for Children's Ministry Elementary Grades

by
Christopher and Gena Maselli (Bible Story Games)
Rod Butler (Situational Games)
Dr. Robert R. Duke (Holiday Games)

Carson-Dellosa Publishing LLC
Greensboro, North Carolina

It is the mission of Carson-Dellosa Christian Education to create the highest-quality Scripture-based children's products that teach the Word of God, share His love and goodness, assist in faith development, and glorify His Son, Jesus Christ.

"...teach me your ways so I may know you...."
Exodus 33:13

Credits

Cover and Layout Design: Nick Greenwood

Cover Photos: © Copyright 1995 Photodisc, Inc. All rights reserved.

© 2007 Jupiterimages Corporation

© 1999 Eyewire, Inc. All rights reserved.

Carson-Dellosa Publishing LLC
PO Box 35665
Greensboro, NC 27425 USA

ISBN 978-1-60418-113-5

02-210131151

Game On!

Give children more than a good time; give them games that will charge their faith! In *180 Faith-Charged Games for Children's Ministry*, you'll find a wide variety of activities, all specially designed to supercharge your teaching.

There are 100 Bible-based games to supplement specific Bible stories or teachings. Ten games provide fun for the holidays, while 70 games are designed to use in special ministry situations. Do you need a quiet game, or one to expel lots of energy? Do you need a game for the activity bus, or one to get new children acquainted? Review the table of contents (page 4–5) for the perfect game for any situation!

Each game is not only tied to a Scripture verse (*Power Source*), but features thought-provoking pre-game and post-game discussion questions. (The pre-game information is titled *Starter* and the post-game material is titled *Power Charge*.) Plus, leaders will love the detailed supply lists (*Power Tools*), playing options (*Alternate Voltage*), and energy meters that show each game's energy level at a glance—from low voltage to high intensity.

Great for large church groups, small classrooms, and everything in between, these *180 Faith-Charged Games* will get your children amped-up with the Word while they're having a blast!

Food Activities:

Caution: Before completing any food activity, ask families' permission and inquire about students' food allergies or other food preferences.

Balloon Activities:

Caution: Before completing any balloon activity, ask families about possible latex allergies. Also, remember that uninflated or popped balloons may present a choking hazard.

Table of Contents

Bible Story Games

Creation. 6
Adam and Eve's Sin. .7
Noah's Ark. 8
The Tower of Babel .9
Abraham 10
Abraham's Test 11
Joseph's Coat 12
Joseph in Prison 13
Joseph and His Brothers 14
Baby Moses. 15
Moses vs. Pharaoh. 16
Parting the Red Sea. 17
Israelites Receive Manna. 18
The Ten Commandments 19
Balaam's Donkey 20
Blessings and Curses. 21
Joshua Enters the Promised Land. 22
Rahab and Israel's Spies 23
The Wall of Jericho 24
Gideon's 300. 25
Samson 26
Ruth and Naomi .27
Samuel Hears God's Call. 28
David and Goliath 29
Jonathan 30
David and Bathsheba 31
Solomon's Choice 32
Elijah Fed by Ravens 33
Elisha and the Widow 34
Zerubbabel Rebuilds the Temple 35
Nehemiah Rebuilds Walls 36
Esther 37
Psalms (Salvation) 38
Psalms (Stillness) .39
Psalms (Angels) .40
Psalms (Praise) 41
Wisdom from Proverbs 42
Proverbs (Trust) 43
Isaiah (God's Word) 44
Isaiah (Strength). 45
The Fiery Furnace 46
Daniel and the Lions' Den. 47
Jonah and the Big Fish 48
Jesus Is Born 49
The Magi Follow the Star 50
Simeon Meets Jesus 51
Jesus as a Boy 52
Twelve-Year-Old Jesus at the Temple 53
John the Baptist .54
Satan Tempts Jesus. 55
Jesus Calls the Disciples 56
The Beatitudes 57
Jesus' Teaching .58
Jesus Turns Water into Wine. 59
Jesus Instructs the Disciples 60
Jesus Anointed by a Sinful Woman. 61
Jesus Calms the Storm 62
Parables of Jesus. 63
The Good Samaritan. 64
Jesus Heals 65
Jesus Feeds 5,000. 66
The 10 Lepers 67
Jesus Blesses the Children 68
The Widow's Giving 69
The Great Commission 70
The Lord's Prayer. 71
Ask, Seek, Knock. 72
Zacchaeus 73
Nicodemus Meets Jesus. 74
Jesus Heals a Paralyzed Man 75
Jesus Raises Lazarus 76
Jesus Enters Jerusalem. 77
Peter and the Fish 78
The Unmerciful Servant. 79
Jesus Clears the Temple 80
Jesus Washes the Disciples' Feet 81
The Parable of the Talents. 82
The Sheep and the Goats. 83
The Last Supper .84
Jesus' Trial and Crucifixion 85
Jesus Appears to Mary 86
Jesus Returns to Heaven. 87
Peter's Vision. 88
Angel Frees Peter from Jail 89
Paul and Silas. 90
Paul's Conversion 91
Paul's Shipwreck .92
Paul's Letters 93
Fruit of the Spirit 94
The Body of Christ 95
Paul's Teaching .96
Paul's Letters 97
Paul Tells Us How to Think 98
Paul Tells Us How to Behave 99
Jesus' Second Coming 100
Paul Instructs Timothy. 101
Hebrews 102
The Teaching of James 103
Overcoming the Enemy 104
Revelation 105

CD-204072 • *180 Faith-Charged Games* • © Carson-Dellosa

Icebreaker Games

God Provides. 106
God Made You Special 107
Your Life Is Deliciously Special 108
In Christ, I Am a New Creation 109
God Knows Us Well. 111
Putting Others First. 112
You Are a Tapestry of God's Design 113
Our Food Comes from God 115
God's Amazing Creation. 116
God Gives Laughter 117

Team-Building Games

The Holy Spirit Helps Us 118
Don't Give Up, Keep Pressing On. 119
God's Power and Majesty 120
The Wonderful Stories of Jesus 121
God Knows Our Thoughts 122
Getting to Know God's Word. 123
Showing Our Faith to Others 124
Shining the Light of Jesus Christ. 125
Working Together 126
Choosing Wisdom. 127

Outdoor Games

Knowing God's Word Makes Me a Winner 128
Seeking God and Counting Blessings 129
God Knows Us Well. 130
Praising the Lord through the Day 131
God Knows Each of Our Thoughts 132
Knowing God's Word Moves Us Forward in Life . 133
We Can Never Hide from God 134
Obeying Parents Promptly 135
Don't Get Close to Sin—Stay Away 136
You Are Important to God 137
Follow Christ's Example 138
All Creation Praises the Lord. 139
Love One Another 140
Perseverance and Patience. 141
Jesus Takes Away Our Sin. 142
What Does Jesus Mean to You? 143
Stay Close to Christ. 144
Keep Praying—Don't Give Up! 145
Walk + Talk = Faith 146
God's Ways Are Higher than Our Ways 147

Silent Games

Helping One Another 148
Obeying God's Word 149
Christians Follow Christ Together 150
God Brings Us Hope 151
Helping One Another 152

Bearing Fruit for Christ 153
Gossip Twists the Truth. 154
God Uses Many Messengers 155
Be Patient 156
The Ten Commandments 157

Games-to-Go

God Made Me. 158
Worship the Lord. 160
When We Seek Him, We Find Him 161
God's Word Has the Answers 162
Seeing God Around Us. 163
All Things Work Together for Good . . . 164
Clap Your Hands in Worship 165
Use Your Talents for God 166
Laughter Is Good for You 167

TV Show Games

Work for the Lord 168
Living Our Lives for the Lord. 169
Truthfulness. 171
God's Word Will See Us to Victory 172
Getting to Know Old Testament Stories 173
Getting to Know New Testament Stories 174
Knowing the Books of the Bible 175
Knowing God's Word Keeps Us Close to God . . . 176
Knowing God's Word Brings Wisdom 177
Growing in God's Word and Ways 178
Seeking the Lord in Prayer and Worship. 179

Holidays and Ancient Traditions

Ancient Olympics 180
The Ancient Game of Kottabos 181
Biblical Poems and Songs. 182
Good Friday/Easter. 183
Christmas. 184
Purim 185
Passover. 186
Rosh Hashanah/Feast of Trumpets 187
Sukkot/Feast of Booths 188
Hanukkah. 189

Appendix 190

Cookie Creations

Energy Level Medium

Starter

This game reminds children just how special they are to God.

Read Genesis 1. Explain to children that God created everything around us. He created space, the planet, the animals, the plants, and every person. He used His wonderful creativity to make each of us unique. Ask children:

- Why do you think God made each person different?
- What makes each person special?

Power Tools

- Baked sugar cookies, one per child
- Colorful icing and sprinkles
- Assorted candies of various shapes, sizes and colors
- Stopwatch

Power Source

So God created man in his own image, in the image of God he created him; male and female he created them. Genesis 1:27

Bible Story Game

Divide into two teams. Announce that each team will have 10 minutes to decorate their cookies. Give awards for each cookie: prettiest, most unusual, tallest, most frosting, best use of color, etc.

Power Charge

Emphasize to the children that just as no two cookies are exactly the same, each child is beautiful and unique. Each child is part of God's creation, and He has special things in store for each of them.

Alternate Voltage

You may choose to have each child draw a cookie shape and decorate it with crayons, glitter, pictures, stickers, etc.

"Pastor Says"

Energy Level Medium

Starter

This game emphasizes obedience. Children will practice listening and obeying quickly.

Read Genesis 3:1–6. Talk about how God gave Adam and Eve everything they would ever need. He told them to stay away from only one thing: a certain tree. Adam and Eve disobeyed God's command and ate a fruit from that tree anyway. The world has never been the same since. Ask children:

- How was Eve deceived into disobeying God?

- Why do you think Adam and Eve disobeyed God?

Power Tools

- None

Power Source

"If you love me, you will obey what I command." John 14:15

Bible Story Game

Have children play the classic game Simon Says. Use your own names in place of Simon. Children should only obey your commands (sit down, stand up, jump, turn around, etc.) when you say, "Pastor Ian says" before the command. If you do not say, "Pastor Ian says," then they should not do what you say. If they follow your command and you haven't said, "Pastor Ian says," then they are eliminated from the game. The last player standing wins.

Power Charge

Explain that God does not want us to follow him without thinking about it. He wants us to choose to follow Him. When He asks us to do something, it is always for our own good. Break into small groups and discuss:

- What are some ways that God wants us to obey Him today?

- What should we do if we disobey God?

Alternate Voltage

For younger players, play Follow the Leader so that they can practice their listening and obeying skills.

Name that Animal Sound

Energy Level
Low

Starter

This game reinforces the story of Noah's ark—recalling God's wonderful provision, protection, and creation as children match animal sounds to their sources.

Read Genesis 6:5–22. Explain that there came a time when people on Earth were so sinful that God sent a flood to destroy them. Mercifully, God protected the good things He had created by saving Noah, his family, and some of the animals. Ask children:

- What made the people of Noah's day so sinful?

- Why do you think God protected Noah, Noah's family, and some of the animals?

Power Tools

- Recording of 10–15 animal sounds (elephant, whale, dolphin, coyote, lion, etc.) Note: Search online for free downloadable animal sounds.

- CD player

- 2 sheets of paper

- 2 pens

Power Source

"You are to bring into the ark two of all living creatures, male and female, to keep them alive with you. . . . " Genesis 6:19

Bible Story Game

Divide into two teams. One at a time, play the recorded animal sounds. Give players 5–10 seconds to write down the animal that they believe is making the sound. The team with the most correct answers wins.

Power Charge

Ask children:

- How did God take care of Noah and his family and the animals during the flood?

- How does God take care of us?

Alternate Voltage

For younger players, create a matching game. Make a worksheet by placing animal pictures in two columns. Make a copy for each child. Have each child mark the picture that correlates to the first sound, second sound, etc.

Mashed Potato Mountain

Energy Level

Medium

Starter

As children build towers in this game, they are reminded of the citizens of Babel who built their tower too—but without consulting the Lord. We are also reminded of how we should always follow God's lead, not our own ideas, in all we do.

Read Genesis 11:1–9. Talk about how the citizens of Babel were so excited by what they could do that they forgot to ask God what He wanted. They tried to build a tower to Heaven to prove how important they were, but God had other plans. He changed their language so that they could not understand each other. This forced them to move to other parts of the world. Ask children:

- Why do you think the people of Babel wanted to build such a big tower?
- Why do you think God stopped them from building the tower?

Power Tools

- Stiff mashed potatoes, enough for each team
- Table
- Ruler
- Stopwatch

Power Source

Then they said, "Come, let us build ourselves a city, with a tower that reaches to the heavens, so that we may make a name for ourselves. . . . " Genesis 11:4

Bible Story Game

Divide into teams of three or four. Announce that teams have two minutes to build a tower of mashed potatoes using only their hands. The team with the tallest tower, as measured by the ruler, wins.

Power Charge

Break into small groups and discuss:

- Why should we ask God for direction in our lives?
- What happens when we don't ask for God's direction in our lives?
- What are some things that we could ask God for direction about this week?

Alternate Voltage

Use play dough instead of potatoes for a less messy option.

Sticker Game

Energy Level
Medium

Starter

God is honorable. When He makes a covenant, it stands forever. This game teaches children not only about Abraham's covenant, but also about our covenant with God through Jesus Christ.

Explain that the word *covenant* means "an unbreakable promise." Then, read Genesis 17:1–8. Remind children that God made this covenant when Abraham was 99 years old. But God kept His Word. Abraham became the father of many nations. God even told him that his offspring would be like the stars—there would be that many of them! Ask children:

- What covenant do we have with God?

- What does that covenant mean to us?

Power Tools

- Sheets of paper with the word *Covenant* written in large, bold print, one per pair

- Star stickers

- Stopwatch

Power Source

"As for me, this is my covenant with you: You will be the father of many nations." Genesis 17:4

Bible Story Game

Divide into pairs. Give each pair a sheet of paper with the word *Covenant* written on it and several sheets of star stickers. Allow teams 30 seconds to peel and stick stars on the letters. When time is up, the team whose sheet has the most stars, and is still legible, wins.

Power Charge

Discuss the covenant that we have with God today. At the end of class, give each child a star sticker as a reminder of that covenant.

Alternate Voltage

If you have extra time, let children play the game again, using the word *Promise*.

Scavenger Hunt

Energy Level

High

Starter

This game's emphasis is on Abraham's test to sacrifice Isaac, and how God was faithful to provide as Abraham was faithful to the end.

Read Genesis 22:1–18. Talk about how God asked Abraham to give up what he loved most: his son Isaac. Ever faithful, Abraham intended to do just that. However, at the last moment, God faithfully substituted a ram in place of Isaac as a sacrifice. Ask children:

- Why do you think God asked Abraham for such a hard sacrifice?
- How difficult do you think this test was for Abraham?

Power Tools

- None

Power Source

To the faithful you show yourself faithful. . . . Psalm 18:25

Bible Story Game

Begin by asking each child to "sacrifice" something, such as a sock or a barrette. Make a list of the items. Then, hide the items around the room. Divide into teams and give each team a list of the items. When you say "Go!" players should search the room for the items on the scavenger hunt list. The first team to find all of its items wins. Return all items to the owners.

Power Charge

Break into small groups and discuss:

- How was your teacher faithful to you during the game?
- How has God shown His faithfulness to you?
- How are you faithful to God?

Alternate Voltage

For an extra challenge, hide items that are open for interpretation, such as "something that shows God's love for you," such as a Bible, a cross, a picture of a rainbow, a glass of water. Allow children to guess why you chose each item.

Clothing Relay

Starter

This game reassures children that God loves them. Just as Joseph's father expressed his love for Joseph by giving him a beautiful coat, God expresses His love by caring for us and accepting us as His children.

Read Genesis 37:3–4. Explain that Joseph's father loved him. To show Joseph how much he cared about him, his father gave him a beautiful coat. In the same way, our Heavenly Father loves us. Because He loves us, He gives us beautiful things too—family, friends, homes, food, clothes, and most importantly, a relationship with Him. Ask children:

- What are some other things that God has given you?

- Why do you think God gives us so many good things?

Power Tools

- 2 boxes

- Large-sized clothes—similar items in each bag or box (hats, men's shirts, men's pants, coats, gloves, men's shoes, etc.)

- Masking tape

Power Source

. . . I am like an olive tree flourishing in the house of God; I trust in God's unfailing love for ever and ever. Psalm 52:8

Bible Story Game

Divide into two teams. Use masking tape to mark a starting and finish line. The first player on each team puts on all of the clothes. He runs to the finish line and back and then gives the clothes to his teammate to put on. The game continues until everyone has had a turn. The first team to get dressed up wins.

Power Charge

Break into small groups and discuss:

- What are some things that God has given you that show His love?

- How can we thank Him for His love?

Potato Puzzle

Energy Level
Medium

Starter

This game uses the story of Joseph to show that we should remain faithful to God even when faced with challenges.

Remind children of Joseph's life—the favor he enjoyed from his father, his brother's jealousy, his slavery, his experience with Potiphar's wife, and his imprisonment. Then read Genesis 39:20–23. Emphasize that, similarly, we may experience difficulties—or puzzles—in our lives, but our challenge is to remain faithful to God like Joseph did, no matter what happens. Ask children:

- Do you think it was easy for Joseph to stand up for what was right?
- What happened to him because he chose to do what was right?
- How did God reward Joseph?

Power Tools

- 2 large, raw baking potatoes cut into 8-10 interlocking puzzle pieces
- Kitchen knife
- Stopwatch

Power Source

But while Joseph was there in the prison, the Lord was with him; he showed him kindness and granted him favor in the eyes of the prison warden. Genesis 39:20–21

Bible Story Game

Show children the assembled potato pieces so that they can see the final result. Then, disassemble the pieces. Time each player. When you say, "Go!" individual players should race to assemble the potato puzzle correctly. The player to complete the puzzle in the shortest amount of time wins.

Power Charge

Break into small groups and discuss:

- In your life, what challenges or puzzles has God helped you solve?
- How did He solve them?

Have children exchange prayer requests with one another. Pray with them as a group, but also ask children to pray for each other during the coming week.

Alternate Voltage

For older children, turn the Power Charge into a journaling exercise.

Pyramid Toss

Energy Level Medium

Starter

This game focuses on the story of Joseph, showing how he forgave his brothers instead of punishing them, and how God turned even the hard parts of his life into good.

Read Genesis 50:15–21. Talk about how Joseph was mistreated by his brothers. Some of his brothers considered killing him, and then sold him as a slave. Years later, Joseph became a very powerful man and had the opportunity to take revenge on his brothers. Instead, he forgave them. Ask children:

- Do you think it was hard for Joseph to forgive his brothers?
- Why do you think Joseph forgave his brothers?

Power Tools

- 9 paper, plastic, or foam cups
- Small rubber ball
- Table

Power Source

. . . we know that in all things God works for the good of those who love Him, who have been called according to His purpose.
Romans 8:28

Bible Story Game

Stack the nine cups in a pyramid shape on a table. Then, explain that Joseph did not try to knock his brothers down, but that they should try and knock down the pyramid. Taking turns, each player should stand five feet (1.5 meters) away from the pyramid and try to knock it down using the ball. Each player gets three tries. The player who knocks down the most cups wins.

Power Charge

Explain that Joseph forgave his brothers for treating him badly. He realized that God used the trouble he went through to bless his family. Break into small groups and discuss:

- What is a bad circumstance you have seen God turn around for good?
- Do you need to forgive someone for a wrongdoing?

Alternate Voltage

Players take turns trying to knock a row of cups off of a table. Whoever knocks the most cups off of the table wins.

Special Purpose Theater

Energy Level Low

Starter

This game recalls that God has a purpose for each of us.

Read Exodus 2:1–10. Talk about how Moses' mother acted in faith and hid Moses. God honored her faith and saved Moses because He had a purpose for him—to free the Israelites. Ask children:

- What made Moses so special that God saved him?
- How early in your life does God have good plans for you?

Power Tools

- Basket
- Strips of paper with jobs written on them (teacher, president, minister, chef, etc.)

Power Source

"For I know the plans I have for you," declares the Lord, "plans to prosper you and not to harm you, plans to give you hope and a future." Jeremiah 29:11

Bible Story Game

Ask children to take turns going to the basket and selecting paper strips. Have each child act out the job on the paper until the rest of the group can guess what they are.

Power Charge

Explain that God has a purpose for each of us and He may lead us to a certain job or life path. He also has a special purpose for us—just like He had for Moses. Break into small groups and discuss:

- What purposes could God have for each person in the group?
- Who are some people that you've seen God use for special purposes—both big and small?

Alternate Voltage

For older children, add more sophisticated "jobs," such as peacemaker, caretaker, aid worker, etc.

Guess the Plagues

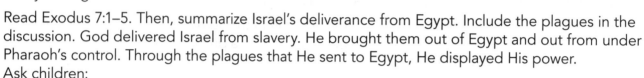

Energy Level
Low

Starter

In this game, children see how far God will go to save His people. Just as He worked to deliver Israel from Pharaoh's injustice, He still delivers His people today through Jesus Christ.

Read Exodus 7:1–5. Then, summarize Israel's deliverance from Egypt. Include the plagues in the discussion. God delivered Israel from slavery. He brought them out of Egypt and out from under Pharaoh's control. Through the plagues that He sent to Egypt, He displayed His power. Ask children:

- What does it mean to be delivered?
- Why did Israel need deliverance?

Power Tools

- Whiteboard or chalkboard
- Markers or chalk
- Hat or bowl
- 10 strips of paper with a different plague written on each: blood, frogs, gnats, flies, animals, boils (or sores), hail, locusts (or grasshoppers), darkness, firstborn
- Stopwatch

Power Source

"'This is what the Lord, the God of the Hebrews, says: Let my people go, so that they may worship me.'" Exodus 9:13

Bible Story Game

Fold the paper strips and place them in the hat. Divide into two teams. Teams should take turns at the board. One player from the team should draw a word from the hat or bowl and then have one minute to draw the item on the board. The player's teammates should try to guess the word. If a team does not guess the word, the other team should use the same clue and take their turn at the board. Team members take turns drawing so that every team member has a turn. The first team to earn six points wins. If the teams tie, choose a word for a tiebreaker. Examples of tiebreaker words are Pharaoh, Moses, and Nile River. For younger players, write the words on the chalkboard.

Power Charge

Ask children:

- How does God deliver us today?
- Who is our deliverer?
- From what are we delivered?

Beanbag Toss

Energy Level High

Starter

This game teaches children that God is ready and willing to deliver them from any trouble.

Read Exodus 14:9–22. Talk about how Moses and the Israelites were being pursued by Pharaoh's armies. When they reached the Red Sea, all seemed lost—they were trapped. God had delivered them from their old lives, but now they needed to be delivered from trouble! The Lord worked a mighty miracle; He parted the waters of the Red Sea for them. Ask children:

- Have you ever felt trapped when trouble came your way?
- How many times will God deliver you?

Power Tools

- Masking tape
- 6–10 beanbags
- Stopwatch

Power Source

. . . "Do not be afraid. Stand firm and you will see the deliverance the Lord will bring you today." Exodus 14:13

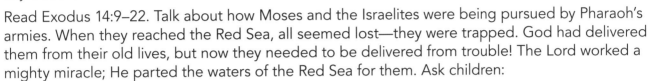

Bible Story Game

Divide into two teams. Place a long strip of masking tape down the center of the "Red Sea" play area, with beanbags on each side. When you say, "Deliver!" each team's players should throw their beanbags over the line to the other team's area. They may also throw beanbags that are tossed into their area back to the other side. When time is up, the team with the smallest number beanbags on their side wins.

Power Charge

Explain that troubles may come our way, big or small, but God will deliver us, just as He delivered us from our old lives. He always has a supernatural plan in mind. Break into small groups. Ask the children if there are any troubles they may need deliverance from now, and then pray for them individually.

Alternate Voltage

Players can also use crumpled paper from the recycling bin.

Confetti Celebration

Energy Level Medium

Starter

This game reminds children that as God provided manna for the Israelites, He will also provide for their needs. Explain to students that the children of Israel wandered in the desert for 40 years after being freed from Egypt. Tell them that the desert is not an easy place to find food, but the Lord took care of them. Every day, God sent a type of bread called manna to rain down from Heaven. The people ate this so that they wouldn't starve.

Read Exodus 16:13–34. Ask children:

- Have you ever had a difficult time in your life—a move, your parents' divorce, a new school, or another major difficulty?

- How did God provide for you through those times?

Power Tools

- Small brown paper bags, one per child
- White confetti
- Red confetti
- Bag of small candies

Power Source

The Lord is good, a refuge in times of trouble. He cares for those who trust in him. Nahum 1:7

Bible Story Game

Fill most bags with red confetti and two with white confetti. Allow each child to select a paper bag. Once every child has a bag, invite them to open their bags. Allow the two children with the white confetti to toss theirs into the air to celebrate. Then, give every child a small piece of candy and remind them that God provides for all.

Power Charge

Give each child a small toy as they leave class. Let the toy serve as a fun reminder that just as God took care of the Israelites during their time in the desert, He will take care of them too.

Alternate Voltage

To make the toys even more special, write the Power Source verse with a marker on each.

Ten Rules to Live By

Starter

This game reinforces the Ten Commandments and the reason God gave them—so that we could understand our need for Him.

Read Exodus 20:1–17. Talk about how God gave His people the commandments and told them they should follow them to the letter—that He was very serious about them. Read through each Commandment one more time and take time to explain what each one means if the children do not understand. Ask children:

- Have you ever broken any of these Commandments?
- Which are the hardest to keep? Why?

Power Tools

- 2 copies of the Ten Commandments written and numbered individually on 10 sheets of paper
- Additional sheets of blank paper
- 2 large trash bags

Power Source

Therefore no one will be declared righteous in his sight by observing the law; rather, through the law we become conscious of sin.
Romans 3:20

Bible Story Game

Divide into two teams. Crumple each paper with a Commandment on it into a ball. Put one copy of each Commandment into each trash bag. Crumple more blank sheets of paper and place them in each trash bag. When you say "I command you to go!" each team should open their trash bag and search through it until they have found all Ten Commandments. They should then place them in order. The first team to do this correctly wins.

Power Charge

Review the Power Source verse. Explain that God gave us the Commandments even though He knew we couldn't keep them. He wanted us to see that we couldn't be perfect on our own—that the only way to be declared good in His sight is to accept Jesus.

Pray a prayer of salvation with the group, letting the children know that if anyone hasn't ever said that they needed Jesus, now's the perfect time!

Alternate Voltage

For older children, use Roman numerals instead of numbers on the papers.

Pin the Teeth on the Donkey

Energy Level Medium

Starter

This game recalls the story of God giving Balaam a warning by making a donkey talk—and it reminds children that God warns us to stay away from evil.

Read Numbers 22:21–35. Talk about how God told Balaam to do something, but Balaam decided to disobey the Lord. He stubbornly went his own way. But before he could get far, God sent a warning—by making Balaam's donkey talk! Ask children:

- What are some ways God warns us of impending danger?

Power Tools

- A donkey's body and head drawn on a poster board
- Blindfold
- Sticky tack
- Drawings of a donkey's teeth (with tape on the back)

Power Source

Balaam answered, "Did I not tell you I should do whatever the Lord says?" Numbers 23:26

Bible Story Game

Have the children play the classic game of Pin the Tail on the Donkey, but instead of the tail, children should pin on its teeth. One by one, have them take turns being blindfolded, spinning, and then attaching the teeth to the donkey. The child who gets the teeth closest to the donkey's mouth wins.

Power Charge

Explain that Balaam heeded God's warning and did exactly what God said. Break into small groups and discuss:

- Why is it important to follow God's orders?
- Why does God warn us?
- Have you ever felt as if God warned you about something? What?

Alternate Voltage

Provide a small reward for children who can say the Power Source verse by memory, while they pin the teeth on the donkey.

Jelly Bean Choices

Energy Level

Low

Starter

This game recalls the blessings and curses God laid out for His people in Deuteronomy and shows that He wants us to choose life.

Read Deuteronomy 30:11–20. In this passage, God made some things very clear to His people: there are blessings and there are curses in life. But more than anything, He wanted them to choose the blessings so that all would go well with them. Ask children:

- What are some of the blessings and curses you heard in those Scriptures?

Power Tools

- Paper bag filled with yellow and red jelly beans

Power Source

. . . I have set before you life and death, blessings and curses. Now choose life. Deuteronomy 30:19

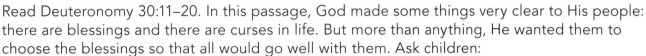

Bible Story Game

Have children taste a yellow and a red jelly bean and vote on which tastes the best. Next, tell children that in this game, yellow jelly beans are good and red jelly beans are evil. Let each child grab one handful of jelly beans from the bag. Allow them to trade with you: two yellow jelly beans for every red jelly bean. The player with the most yellow jelly beans wins.

Power Charge

Explain that God has laid it out before us—we can choose His blessings or the enemy's curses. We have the opportunity each and every day—at home, at school, and elsewhere—to choose blessings. Break into small groups and discuss:

- When did you recently have an opportunity to choose between a blessing and a curse?
- Why do you think God so strongly states that He wants us to choose blessings?

Alternate Voltage

For another option, choose common flavors such as cherry, strawberry, and banana. For a unique experience, choose flavors such as popcorn, root beer, and key lime pie.

Move the Stones

Starter

Joshua's entry into the promised land is a great reminder that God fulfills His promise to take care of us, and we should honor Him for that.

Remind children of the significance of Israel entering the Promised Land. To commemorate the event, God told them to do something very specific. Read Joshua 4:1–9. Ask children:

- Why do you think God asked Joshua to set up the stones?
- Why is it important to remember the good things in our lives?

Power Tools

- 40 toy bricks or blocks
- Masking tape

Power Source

I will remember the deeds of the Lord; yes, I will remember your miracles of long ago. Psalm 77:11

Bible Story Game

Divide into two teams. Set up two piles of toy bricks, 20 per pile, in the center of the room. Explain that players should race from their team's starting lines (marked with masking tape) to their pile of bricks. Taking one brick at a time, each player should return to his team's starting line and place the brick behind it. Then, the next player should race back to the pile to retrieve another brick. Each team should continue until all of their bricks are restacked behind the line. The first team to completely restack all of its bricks wins.

Power Charge

Break into small groups and discuss:

- How can we honor God every day?
- What are some things you want to honor God for?

Alternate Voltage

Write one word of the Power Source verse and its reference on each of the bricks. Ask the children to stack the bricks in order.

The Writing Is on the Wall

Energy Level

Medium

Starter

Just as God had a plan for Israel, He has a plan for each of us. This game emphasizes the importance of following God's plan in our lives.

Read Joshua 2. Explain that God directed Joshua to send spies into Jericho to learn how to secure the land for the Israelites. God had a plan to give Israel the land. He used Rahab to protect the spies. In return, Israel protected Rahab and her family. Ask children:

- Has God shown you that He has a specific plan for your life?

- What are some things God has directed you to do?

Power Tools

- Paper
- Alphabet Code written on paper (see page 190), one per team
- 2 pairs of binoculars
- 2 pencils
- Masking tape

Power Source

. . . "I know that the Lord has given this land to you." Joshua 2:9

Bible Story Game

Write the Alphabet Code on two sheets of paper. Print the following numeric phrase on two sheets of paper: 4, 15, 6, 9, 22, 5, 10, 21, 13, 16, 9, 14, 7, 10, 1, 3, 11, 19. (Answer: Do five jumping jacks.) The numbers should be small enough that using the binoculars is necessary to read them from across the room. (Note: Test the binoculars beforehand to make sure that the numbers are readable.) Tape the paper to a wall at the back of the room.

Divide into two teams. Explain that one player from each team should use the binoculars to read the numbers. The other players should record the numbers and use the code at the top of the paper to decipher the phrase. Once they have deciphered the phrase, all players should do what the phrase tells them. The first team to decipher the phrase and perform five jumping jacks wins.

Power Charge

Pray corporately for God's plans to be completed in the children's lives. Ask the Lord to show them how they can best accomplish the plans He has for them.

Alternate Voltage

For increased difficulty, use symbols instead of numbers or add a second phrase for children to decipher and complete.

Jericho March

Energy Level
Medium

Starter

This game recalls the story of Joshua marching around Jericho and reminds children that it is always better to follow God's plans than their own.

Read Joshua 6:1–20. Talk about how God gave Joshua a command: march around the city of Jericho, with his army, once each day for six days—and on the seventh day, they were to march around it seven times and then blow their trumpets. If they did this, the Lord said the wall of Jericho would fall. Ask children:

- Does this sound like a good battle plan? Is that the way wars are usually fought?
- Why do you think Joshua decided it was a good plan?

Power Tools

- Pull-string piñata
- Candy, pennies, or other small gifts
- 7 strips of paper, numbered individually 1–7
- Clear tape

Power Source

By faith the walls of Jericho fell, after the people had marched around them for seven days. Hebrews 11:30

Bible Story Game

Follow the piñata's directions to fill it with candy, pennies, or gifts. Tape each strip of paper to the piñata strings, making sure to attach the 7 strips to the string that will open the piñata. Divide into seven teams. After teams 1–6 each march around the room once, the leader of each team should pull her team's string. Team 7 should march around the room seven times and then pull the seventh string. When the piñata opens, players can dive for the treasure.

Power Charge

Explain that the battle plan worked for Joshua because it was God's plan. It didn't matter how strange it seemed; because God said it, it would work. The challenge was for Joshua to have faith in what God said and not to do things the way he was used to doing them. Ask the children to share something God has asked them to do that is different than the way they would have done it themselves.

Alternate Voltage

Have children say the Power Source verse before pulling their string. You could also have a child blow a harmonica or birthday blower to simulate the trumpets blowing after each march.

Human Tic-Tac-Toe

Starter

This game relates the story of Gideon and his army and how God used a most unusual way to defeat the enemy—a way Gideon would have never guessed.

Read Judges 7:1–8, 16–21. Talk about how Gideon was leading an army of 32,000 men. He went to fight the enemy, but before he did, God told him to send all of the soldiers home except for 300! Then when they went to fight, they used their voices, trumpets, and lanterns against the enemy. It's not what Gideon would have planned. Ask children:

- How was God's plan different from what Gideon's would probably have been?

- How successful was God's way?

Power Tools

- 9 chairs, set in 3 rows of 3

Power Source

"For my thoughts are not your thoughts, neither are your ways my ways," declares the Lord. "As the heavens are higher than the earth, so are my ways higher than your ways and my thoughts than your thoughts." Isaiah 55:8–9

Bible Story Game

With the chairs in a tic-tac-toe pattern, have four boys and four girls stand 5 feet (1.5 meters) away from the chairs. Boys are X's; girl's are O's. Explain that when you say, "Go!" they should race to sit in a chair (one chair should be left empty each time). The team with three seats in a row wins. Play best four out of five games. Notice as you begin, children almost always race to their seats. But as they play more, they should begin to realize strategy, not racing, guarantees the win.

Power Charge

Explain that many times we try to do things our own way—just like when we first started playing Human Tic-Tac-Toe. But as we discovered, it took stopping and thinking to win—not just racing. It's like that in life; we should be willing to stop and pray and ask God to give us the best strategy. Break into small groups and discuss:

- What are some areas of life in which God wants us to win?

- What are some ways He has given us to win?

Alternate Voltage

If your group does not have a good mix of boys and girls, to assign teams, give each child a sheet of paper with an X or O written on it.

Bowling for Pillars

Energy Level Medium

Starter

Recalling the story of Samson, children will learn that their strength—strength of spirit, mind and body—comes from their Heavenly Father.

Tell children the story of Samson. Remind them of his birth, his position of authority, and his strength. Relate the story of Delilah. Read Judges 16:23–31. Ask children:

- What does it mean to be strong physically?
- How does a person grow stronger physically?

Power Tools

- 3 pillars (bowling pins, stacks of blocks or other pillar-like materials)
- Rubber or plastic ball
- Masking tape

Power Source

"The Lord is my strength and my song; he has become my salvation." Exodus 15:2

Bible Story Game

Divide into two teams. Set up three pillars in a triangle shape at one end of the playing area. At the other end of the area, mark a starting line with masking tape. Players from each team should try to knock down the pillars by bowling the ball toward them. Each player gets two tries to knock down the pillars. Award one point for each toppled pillar. The team with the most points wins.

Power Charge

Break into small groups and discuss:

- What does it mean to be strong spiritually, to be strong inside?
- How can a person grow stronger spiritually?

Alternate Voltage

Schedule a bowling outing for children. Contact a local bowling alley to find out if they offer group discounts. Have parents drop off their children for an hour of fun. Tie it into this lesson by calling it *Samson's Bowl-a-thon: How many pillars can you knock down?* When preparing the information sheets and permission slips for parents, include questions from Power Charge that parents can discuss with their children to reinforce the lesson.

Fill Us Up

Energy Level High

Starter

This game reminds us that God fills our spiritual bowls when we are faithful. God always rewards faithfulness. Just as He rewarded Ruth for her faithfulness to Naomi, He will reward our faithfulness too. Remind children of the great honor that God gave to Ruth: even though she was not Jewish, she became a great-grandmother to King David and, therefore, a part of Jesus' genealogy.

Read the book of Ruth and summarize the story for children. Ask children:

- Why is faithfulness so important?
- How does God reward faithfulness?

Power Tools

- 2 large buckets
- Several bags of birdseed
- 2 small paper or foam cups
- 2 identical bowls
- Masking tape

Power Source

"May the Lord repay you for what you have done. May you be richly rewarded by the Lord, the God of Israel, under whose wings you have come to take refuge."
Ruth 2:12

Bible Story Game

Divide into two teams and go outside. Place equal amounts of birdseed in each bucket, Then, place the buckets at one end of the playing area. On the other end of the area, mark a starting line with masking tape and place the bowls on the line. Players should take turns racing to their bucket of seed, filling their cup, returning to their bowl, and dumping the seed into their team's bowls. The first team to fill their bowl wins.

Power Charge

Using a chalkboard, dry erase board, or a poster board and markers, allow children to suggest how they can be faithful in the coming week. Ask children:

- What are some ways that we can be faithful to others around our own house (cleaning my room, setting the table for dinner, doing homework without being asked, etc.)?
- Next week, review the list and ask children how they stayed faithful.

Alternate Voltage

For an added challenge, have the players use spoons instead of cups.

Obey the Voice

Starter

Recalling the story of Samuel and Eli, this game serves as a reminder that it's important to listen for God's direction in all we do.

Read 1 Samuel 3:1–10. Explain to children that, at first, Samuel didn't know that God was speaking to him. Samuel had to learn to listen to Him. In the same way, we should learn to listen and obey God's voice. Ask children:

- Have you ever heard God's voice or known that He was telling you to do something?
- How did He speak to you?
- Did you obey Him?

Power Tools

- 2 blindfolds
- 2 identical obstacle courses using chairs, blocks, or other items that serve as obstacles around which the players should maneuver

Power Source

The Lord came and stood there, calling as at the other times, "Samuel! Samuel!" Then Samuel said, "Speak, for your servant is listening." 1 Samuel 3:10

Bible Story Game

Divide into pairs. In each pair, one player should be blindfolded and the other should give directions. When the game begins, players should guide the blindfolded players through the obstacle course using only verbal instructions. The guiding players may not touch the blindfolded players. The first pair to complete the obstacle course correctly wins.

Power Charge

Give each child a piece of paper and a pen. Have them record a personal need that requires God's direction (school, friends, parents, etc.). Then, ask them to pray. Have each child write how God has directed her. Next week, ask the children to share how God directed them and what they did.

Alternate Voltage

If space is an issue, have teams take turns going through the course and using a stopwatch to determine a winner. Make sure to isolate the second team so that they don't gain an unfair advantage by watching the first team.

G-O-L-I-A-T-H

Energy Level High

Starter

This game reminds children that God will defend them whenever trouble arises.

Summarize the story of David and Goliath in 1 Samuel 17. Explain to children that David was not the most likely person to fight Goliath, but he had one very important thing going for him—he trusted God. Then, read verses 40-50. Ask children:

- Had David trained to be a soldier when he fought Goliath?
- What made him different from the other soldiers of Israel?

Power Tools

- Mini basketball
- Mini basketball hoop
- Masking tape

Power Source

"All those gathered here will know that it is not by sword or spear that the Lord saves; for the battle is the Lord's, and He will give all of you into our hands."
1 Samuel 17:47

Bible Story Game

Divide into two teams. Explain that they will be playing a variation on the basketball game Horse. Each player should take turns shooting a basket from a free throw line (marked with masking tape). Each time a team member makes a basket, another letter is added to that team's score until one team spells GOLIATH. The first team to spell GOLIATH wins.

Power Charge

Break into small groups and discuss:

- Have you ever asked God to be your defender?

Reassure children that God can and will defend them. Like He did for David, He will give them wisdom on how to handle situations that would hurt their bodies, minds, or spirits. Then ask:

- Does anyone need us to pray for God to defend him? Is anyone facing a dangerous or hurtful situation that requires God's help?

Take prayer requests from those who need protection. Be sure to listen for serious requests that may need special attention.

Alternate Voltage

For an outing or if facilities are available, use a full-size basketball hoop.

Three-Legged Race

Starter

This game emphasizes the importance of unity as it recalls the friendship of David and Jonathan.

Read 1 Samuel 20:1–17. Explain to the children that David and Jonathan were good friends. The Bible says that Jonathan loved David as much as he loved himself. Their friendship helped save David from Saul, Jonathan's father. They worked together, and that unity made them a mighty force.

Ask children:

- Why is friendship important?
- Can you accomplish more in life with or without friends?

Power Tools

- Length of rope
- Masking tape
- Chairs

Power Source

. . . "Go in peace, for we have sworn friendship with each other in the name of the Lord."
1 Samuel 20:42

Bible Story Game

Divide into pairs and go outside. For this three-legged race, each player should tie one leg to a teammate's leg. Starting from the starting/finish line marked with masking tape, children should race across the course, around the chair, and back to the starting/finish line. The first team to finish wins.

Power Charge

Ask children:

- What does the word *unity* mean?
- How can we have unity with others?
- Why is unity important?

Alternate Voltage

For a more challenging game, create a more difficult obstacle course.

Cover Up

Starter

In this game based on the story of David and Bathsheba, children will learn that sin has a price.

Reacquaint yourself with the story of David and Bathsheba, 2 Samuel 11–12. Summarize it for children. Let children know that sin can be tempting, but explain that when we allow sin into our lives, we set up ourselves for heartache because sin ruins everything it touches.

Ask children:

- What should David have done when he found out that Bathsheba was married?
- What happened when David tried to cover up his sin?

Power Tools

- White sheet of paper, one per child
- Crayons and markers
- Masking tape and transparent tape
- White correction pens
- Poster board

Power Source

For the wages of sin is death, but the gift of God is eternal life in Christ Jesus our Lord.
Romans 6:23

Bible Story Game

Have each child draw a picture of something that he has done that is wrong (hitting, talking back, etc.). Collect the pictures and tape them in a collage on poster board. Then, have children use masking tape, white correction pens, and paper to cover the pictures of sins. Solicit volunteers to interpret what they've done by covering the pictures. Explain that covering up does not make something clean again. Only God can do that. Have each child draw a new picture that shows a good example. The child who makes the correction first wins.

Power Charge

Ask children what sin is and how they feel after they have sinned. Explain that God forgives sins when we confess our sins to Him. Pray with children who want forgiveness for sin. Have leaders available in case any child would like to talk to someone in more depth.

Alternate Voltage

Write the Power Source verse on strips of paper with as a reminder of today's lesson and give one to each child. If time allows, decorate the paper strips with Christian stickers. For young children you may wish to leave off "For the wages of sin is death."

Wisdom Blast

Energy Level Low

Starter

In this game, children will learn about Solomon's choice to receive wisdom from God, as well as discover some of His wise proverbs.

Read 1 Kings 4:29–34. Talk about how God told Solomon he could ask for anything. Relate how Solomon asked for wisdom and how this greatly pleased the Lord, who not only gave him unmatched wisdom, but also great riches, honor, and long life. (1 Kings 3:13–14)

Ask children:

• What would you ask for if God said you could have anything?

Power Tools

• Favorite proverbs, written on small strips of paper

• Silly sayings, written on small strips of paper (Prepare two proverbs for each silly saying.)

• Hat

Power Source

. . . the Lord appeared to Solomon during the night in a dream, and God said, "Ask for whatever you want me to give you." 1 Kings 3:5

Bible Story Game

Place the proverbs and silly sayings into a hat and shuffle them together. One at a time, allow each child to select a paper strip from the hat and read it aloud. The other children should give the "thumbs-up" sign if they think that it is a real proverb or the "thumbs-down" sign if they think that it is just a silly saying. After the children have guessed, share each correct answer.

Power Charge

Explain why it pleases the Lord so much when Solomon asks for wisdom. [This was a selfless request so that he could rule God's people well (1 Kings 3:7–9).] Take time to pray together, asking God to forgive our selfishness and to give us wisdom at home, at school, and with friends.

Alternate Voltage

Play the game so that if a child incorrectly identifies a silly saying as a proverb (or vice versa), it results in a point for the other player.

Cotton Drop

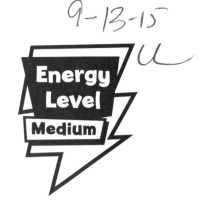

Energy Level Medium

9-13-15

Starter

This game recalls the story of Elijah being fed by ravens, demonstrating God's never-ending ability to meet the needs of His people.

Read 1 Kings 17:2–6. Talk about how Elijah was doing what God told him to do, but that made King Ahab angry. Elijah had to run away to stay safe. But, how would he live away from the city and not go hungry? God provided a miracle: He had ravens bring Elijah food. Ask children:

- Why do you think God used birds to feed Elijah?
- What do you think Elijah learned from this?

Power Tools

- Drinking straws, one per child (not bendable type)
- Large cotton balls, one per child

Power Source

And my God will meet all your needs according to His glorious riches in Christ Jesus.
Philippians 4:19

Bible Story Game

Divide into two teams. Give each team member a straw. Give each team captain his team's cotton balls. When you shout, "Elijah's hungry!" players should take turns using their straws (no hands allowed) to transfer a cotton ball from one player to another. Children attach the cotton ball to the end of the straw by inhaling with their mouths. The first team to transfer all of its cotton balls to the last player in line wins.

Power Charge

Explain that the relay in this game was like the ravens in the story of Elijah. They transferred "food" from one place to another when asked. Break into small groups and discuss:

- How might God transfer your needs to you?
- Can God supply any need you might have?

Alternate Voltage

Create a large pile of cotton balls and use a stopwatch to time individual children. The player to transfer the most cotton balls from the large pile to the final destination in a specified time wins.

Oil Transfer

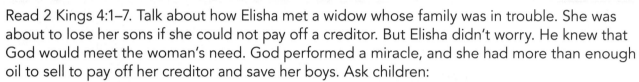

Energy Level Medium

Starter

This game reinforces the story of Elisha helping the widow save her family, recalling God's desire and ability to provide for families.

Read 2 Kings 4:1–7. Talk about how Elisha met a widow whose family was in trouble. She was about to lose her sons if she could not pay off a creditor. But Elisha didn't worry. He knew that God would meet the woman's need. God performed a miracle, and she had more than enough oil to sell to pay off her creditor and save her boys. Ask children:

- Does God still perform miracles to meet our families' needs today?

Power Tools

- 2 bowls of vegetable oil
- 2 empty measuring cups
- 2 teaspoons
- Stopwatch

Power Source

. . . your Father knows what you need before you ask him. Matthew 6:8

Bible Story Game

Divide into two teams. One player at a time from each team should transfer oil from a bowl into a measuring cup using a teaspoon. The team that reaches the designated measurement on the cup first wins.

Power Charge

Explain that God knows our needs before we ask Him. We can trust Him, knowing that He will take care of our families. Even when it seems impossible, the God of Elisha will come through. Break into small groups and discuss:

- If God knows our family's needs, why does He want us to pray about them?
- What are some needs your family has that you can ask God to meet?

Alternate Voltage

To make the game harder or easier, change the size of the spoon and the distance between the bowl and the measuring cup.

Rebuild The Temple

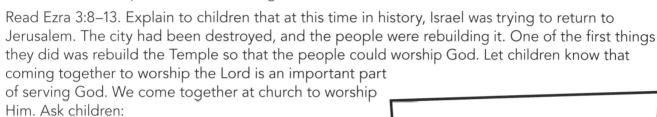

Energy Level

High

Starter

The Lord loves it when we come together to worship Him. In this game, children will discover the importance of attending church.

Read Ezra 3:8–13. Explain to children that at this time in history, Israel was trying to return to Jerusalem. The city had been destroyed, and the people were rebuilding it. One of the first things they did was rebuild the Temple so that the people could worship God. Let children know that coming together to worship the Lord is an important part of serving God. We come together at church to worship Him. Ask children:

- Why was it important for Israel to rebuild the Temple?

- How is the Temple like our church?

Power Tools

- 3 sets of 15 empty soda cans, numbered 1 to 15

Power Source

Let us not give up meeting together, as some are in the habit of doing, but let us encourage one another—and all the more as you see the Day approaching.
Hebrews 10:25

Bible Story Game

Divide into two teams. Assemble one set of cans in a pyramid formation in the middle of the room. Tell children that this represents the Temple. Make sure that the numbers on the cans are visible. It is not necessary for the numbers to be in order. In fact, it will add a level of difficulty if they are not in order. At the start of the game, both teams should work to assemble their cans in a pyramid formation with the numbers on their cans in the same order as the center pyramid. The first team to build their pyramid correctly wins.

Power Charge

When the foundation of the Temple was laid, the people were so happy that they shouted and wept. Break into small groups and discuss:

- Why is it important to attend church?

- What is your favorite thing about church?

Alternate Voltage

Listen to children during the small group time. This is a great time to talk to them about ways to improve your children's church ministry.

Wall Builder

Energy Level High

Starter

In this game, children will see that God gave Nehemiah a plan to rebuild Jerusalem's walls and bring honor back to the holy city. In the same way, God gives us plans and purposes for our lives.

Summarize the story of Israel's exile and the state of Jerusalem in Nehemiah's time. Read Nehemiah 2:11–20. Nehemiah was faithful to do what God asked. He followed God's plan and rebuilt the walls in only 52 days. Ask children:

- What did God tell Nehemiah?
- Why do you think it was so important to repair the walls around Jerusalem?

Power Tools

- 30 empty soda cans
- Stopwatch

Power Source

Commit to the Lord whatever you do, and your plans will succeed. Proverbs 16:3

Bible Story Game

Divide into two teams. Give each team 15 cans. Each team should stack as many cans as possible, one on top of another, to rebuild Jerusalem's walls. The team that stacks more cans, with the cans remaining securely in place for at least 10 seconds, wins. Teams can take turns or can stack their cans at the same time.

Power Charge

Give each child a can of juice or punch as they leave class. Attach a small note with today's Power Source verse on it. Let this serve as a reminder that God has important plans for each of them.

Alternate Voltage

When counting the seconds that the cans stay in place, allow the children to count aloud for added excitement.

Treasure Hunt

Energy Level High

Starter

This game reinforces the story of Esther and how God rewarded her obedience.

Summarize the story of Esther for children and read Esther 4:12–16. Explain that Esther was an obedient woman. She obeyed Mordecai, therefore saving her family and helping to bring deliverance to the Jewish people. Ask children:

- Why is obedience so important?
- Whom should we obey?

Power Tools

- 2 sets of treasure hunt clues, 5 in each set (see page 190)
- Treasure (candy, restaurant coupons, small toys, etc.)
- Decorated shoe box (to hold treasure)

Power Source

If you fully obey the Lord your God and carefully follow all His commands I give you today, the Lord your God will set you high above all the nations on earth. Deuteronomy 28:1

Bible Story Game

Divide into two teams. Create a treasure hunt for each team. The hunts should be similar in content. Players should decipher clues in order, "obediently" following directions, to help them find the location of the next clue. The last clue should lead them to the treasure. For example, I like to sit in the back (under a chair in the last row).

Power Charge

As God's children, we are called to be obedient and follow rules. First, we must be obedient to God, and then we must be obedient to those who have authority over us—our parents, the government, our teachers, and our bosses. Teach children that while it is important to respect authority, there will also be times when people in authority will try to pull them away from God or have them do bad things. Help children distinguish the difference. As a class, discuss:

- When should we obey?
- When should we not obey?

Alternate Voltage

For older children, create rhyming clues and to make them more difficult. For younger children, use picture clues.

Name that Baby Food

Energy Level Low

Starter

This game, based on a verse in Psalms, is a call to salvation for those children who still need to experience it.

Read Psalm 34:8. Point out that David was a child when he was called by God to be king of Israel, David was the youngest son of many children, King Saul tried to have David killed, David committed sins, and he ended up hurting himself. Ask children:

- What do you think King David meant when he wrote that verse?
- How do we "taste and see that the Lord is good"?

Power Tools

- 4 jars of baby food with the labels removed, numbered 1–4 (fruits are recommended)
- Paper plate for each child divided into quarters, numbered 1–4
- Plastic spoons
- 2 blindfolds

Power Source

Taste and see that the Lord is good; blessed is the man who takes refuge in him. Psalm 34:8

Bible Story Game

Spoon a small amount of baby food into the appropriate quadrant of each child's plate. Each player should taste the baby food saying, "Taste and see that the Lord is good" before they sample it. They they should try to guess what they are tasting. The player who correctly identifies the most foods wins.

Power Charge

Explain that in the game children tasted with their taste buds. In the Scripture, they taste when they open their hearts and experience God. Have a time of prayer and open the opportunity for children to pray a prayer of salvation.

Alternate Voltage

For an easier game, use differing flavors like peas and bananas. Combine flavors like apples and sweet potatoes to make the game more challenging.

Freeze Play

Starter

This game focuses on the importance of being still and knowing God.

Read Psalm 46. Then, reread verse 10. Talk about how we get busy in life with school, friends, and sports. But sometimes we need to take time to be quiet because God often uses quiet times to speak to us. Ask children:

• What other things distract us from being still and quiet?

Power Tools

• Music CD
• CD player

Power Source

"Be still, and know that I am God." Psalm 46:10

Bible Story Game

Explain to the children that this game is about being still. Encourage them to dance, march, twirl, or sing when music is played. When the music stops, they should all freeze in place and stand perfectly still. Anyone who moves or makes a sound is out. The last child standing wins.

Power Charge

Explain that God wants us to have fun. He wants us to laugh, run, dance, and play. But there are times when we should stop everything and listen for Him speaking to our spirits. Sing a soft worship song, such as the song "Still, Still, Still" and take a short time to be quiet together and listen for God's message to us. Afterward, ask children to share if they feel that God spoke to them.

Alternate Voltage

Encourage children to be extra silly during musical moments, thus making their classmates laugh when they're supposed to be frozen.

Aim and Protect

Starter

This game helps children understand that God sends angels to protect them and help them in their lives.

Read Psalm 91:9–13. Explain that angels are special beings created by God. They serve as messengers, helpers, and protectors. Ask children:

- What do you think of when you hear the word *angels*?

- What do angels do for us today?

Power Tools

- Masking tape
- 2 large toy hoops
- Small foam balls
- Stopwatch

Power Source

For he will command his angels concerning you to guard you in all your ways. Psalm 91:11

Bible Story Game

Divide into two teams. Use masking tape to create a line down the middle of the playing area. Each team should stand on one side of the line and should not cross the line. Each team should consist of one protected player; the other players should be protectors. Place the hoops 4–6 feet (1–2 meters) away from the line on each side. The protected player should remain inside the hoop. Each team's protectors have two goals: they should use the foam balls to try to hit the other team's protected player, and they should protect their own player by swatting away the foam balls that are thrown toward him. At the end of three minutes, the team that has hit the other team's protected player the most wins.

Power Charge

Ask children to share times when they know God protected them, perhaps by sending angels.

Alternate Voltage

Invite an adult from your church into the service to share a time when God protected her.

Name That Tune

Energy Level
Low

Starter

This game emphasizes why the Psalms were written and why it is important to sing to the Lord.

Read Psalm 150. Talk about how God is worthy to be praised for so many reasons and in so many ways. One way we worship God is by singing songs to Him and writing songs to Him. Every one of the 150 chapters in the book of Psalms is a song written to praise the Lord! Ask children:

- Do you know any songs about the Lord? Tell us or sing part of one to us.

Power Tools

- Music CD
- CD player

Power Source

Let everything that has breath praise the Lord. Psalm 150:6

Bible Story Game

Play a portion of a familiar song sung in the children's church or a popular Christian song. Explain that at any point during the music, players can raise their hands and say "Got it" to signify that they know the song. At that point, stop the music and allow the player to identify the tune. If she is correct, she gets a point. If she is incorrect, another player may guess or the music continues until another player says "Got it." The player with the most points after a preset time wins.

Power Charge

Talk about how every song sung in church was written by someone. Someone thought that his song would be a good way to worship the Lord. Sing a worshipful psalm together.

Alternate Voltage

If any children play instruments or write music, ask them to present a song to the class.

Hop with Me!

Starter

This game shares the truth that God directs our steps when we submit ourselves to Him.

Read Proverbs 3:1–8. Talk about how God does not want us to feel like we are alone in this life, trying to decide what to do. He wants to lead us, guide us, and show us the way. And when we trust God, Scripture says He will direct our steps. Ask children:

- When is a time you know God directed your steps or the steps of someone you love?

Power Tools

- Masking tape
- Blindfold

Power Source

The steps of a good man are ordered by the Lord, and He delights in His way.
Psalm 37:23 nkjv

Bible Story Game

Divide into pairs. Mark an unpredictable hopscotch pattern on the floor. One teammate should wear the blindfold as the other directs his partner to properly jump the hopscotch. The other teams should cheer for everyone's hopper. Everyone wins at this game.

Power Charge

Explain that God will speak directly to our hearts if we listen for Him when we pray. He also speaks to us through His Word and through those who follow Him. If we are ever unsure if we are truly hearing His direction, we should compare what we heard to what the Bible says—it is the standard for everything. Break into small groups and discuss:

- Have you been looking for an answer to a problem? What might God be saying to you? What steps can you take to hear from God and then follow His direction?

Alternate Voltage

Complete the game outside and use chalk to draw hopscotch squares on the ground.

Twists and Turns

Energy Level
Medium

Starter

This game reminds us that when we trust in the Lord, not ourselves, He will guide us.

Read Proverbs 3:5–6. Talk about how many times we try to do things on our own, but if we put our trust in God instead, it will make a world of difference! When we give God the glory in all we do, our paths will be straight. Ask children:

- When is a time you trusted God and it worked out well for you?

Power Tools

- A remote-controlled car
- Obstacles (blocks, cones, etc.)
- Stopwatch

Power Source

Trust in the Lord with all your heart and lean not on your own understanding; in all your ways acknowledge him, and He will make your paths straight.
Proverbs 3:5–6

Bible Story Game

Create an obstacle course for a remote-controlled car. Taking turns, allow each child to race the car through the obstacles and back. The player who completes the course in the shortest time wins.

Power Charge

Explain that life has twists and turns—but there is One who knows every turn and desires to make our paths straight. All it takes is putting our faith and trust in Him. Break into small groups and discuss:

- What are ways you can trust God in what you do?
- How do you acknowledge God in your activities?

Alternate Voltage

Increase or decrease the challenge by adding or taking away obstacles in the course.

Yo-Yo Competition

Starter

In this game, children learn the importance and power of God's Word. They will learn that they can trust it, cling to it, and build their lives upon it.

Tell children that God has always had a plan for the nation of Israel. He wants them to cling to Him and His Word, and He promised them that His Word would not return empty. Explain that the prophet Isaiah lived during a time when part of Israel, called Judah, had turned its back on the Lord. Then read Isaiah 55. Ask children:

- Why is it so important to know God's Word?
- What does God mean when He says that his word "will not return to me empty"?

Power Tools

- 5 yo-yos

Power Source

"So is my word that goes out from my mouth: It will not return to me empty, but will accomplish what I desire and achieve the purpose for which I sent it." Isaiah 55:11

Bible Story Game

Divide into groups of five. Allow players to practice with the yo-yos before the game begins. Allow each group to compete to find the player who can yo-yo the longest.

Power Charge

Today, we played with yo-yos. The purpose of a yo-yo is to return to where it started. Sometimes, though, the yo-yo falters. It does not do what it is supposed to do, but God's Word always does. We can trust God's Word because it stands forever. Break into small groups and discuss:

- How can we respect God's Word?
- How should we study the Bible?

Alternate Voltage

For those good at yo-yoing, challenge them to say Isaiah 55:11 as they play.

Soaring Like Eagles

Energy Level Medium

Starter

This game recalls the comforting words of Isaiah and teaches children that putting hope in the Lord will renew their strength.

Read Isaiah 40:28–31. Talk about how God does not grow tired, and He can help us when we get tired. If we put our hope in Him, our strength will be renewed. Ask children:

- What does the Bible mean when it says we will "soar on wings like eagles"?

Power Tools

- Sheets of paper, one per child

Power Source

. . . those who hope in the Lord will renew their strength. They will soar on wings like eagles; they will run and not grow weary, they will walk and not be faint. Isaiah 40:31

Bible Story Game

Have each child fold her paper into an airplane. Allow children to take turns throwing their airplanes, trying to make them soar as far as they can. Whoever's plane soars the farthest wins. Challenge students to design different airplanes and see which design is most successful.

Power Charge

Explain that God has called each of us to great things, and He does not want us to grow weary before we finish them. When we get tired, we need to look to God for the answers, trusting Him to give us strength to do whatever He has planned next for us. Break into small groups and discuss:

- What does it mean to put your hope in the Lord?
- What are some things you're hoping for today?

Alternate Voltage

For a longer game, give players multiple opportunities to fly their planes and take the best of their throws.

10/11

Chasing Away the Flames

Energy Level

High

Starter

Through the story of Shadrach, Meshach, and Abednego, children will learn that they must submit to God's authority above all else.

Remind children of the story of Shadrach, Meshach, and Abednego in Daniel 3. Talk about the positions they held, the choice they had to make, and the consequences they faced. Above all, make it clear that because they bowed to God and not an idol, God saved them from the fiery furnace. Ask children:

- Was it easy for Shadrach, Meshach, and Abednego to obey God instead of the king?
- How did God protect them?

Power Tools

- 2 red balloons
- 2 paper plates
- Cone (or chair)
- Masking tape

Power Source

"If we are thrown into the blazing furnace, the God we serve is able to save us from it, and he will rescue us from your hand, O king." Daniel 3:17

Bible Story Game

Divide into two teams. One member of each team should begin at the starting line (marked with masking tape). Using a paper plate, each player should fan a balloon across the playing area, around the cone at the far end, and back to the starting line. Then, he should hand his paper plate to his teammate, who should complete the course. The players may not touch or move the balloon with anything except the breeze that they create with their plates. The first team to cross the finish line wins.

Power Charge

At the end of class, give a red balloon to each child. Tell children that these balloons represent the decisions that they will make this week. They must choose to submit to God in everything. It is the only way that they will truly be able to chase the flames away!

Alternate Voltage

Follow up next week by asking children if they were faced with a choice to follow their own ways or God's.

- What choices did they make?
- Were the decisions easy or difficult?

Feed the Lions

Starter

Through the story of Daniel and the lion's den, children will discover that having faith in God is rewarding. Daniel's faith kept him safe in the lion's den. God sealed the lions' mouths shut.

Remind children of Daniel's position in the government and of his character. Read Daniel 6. Ask children:

- What made Daniel different from the other men in King Darius' government?
- Why is having faith in God so important?
- How did others respond to Daniel?

Power Tools

- 2 bowls or bags of popcorn
- Masking tape

Power Source

My shield is God Most High, who saves the upright in heart.
Psalm 7:10

Bible Story Game

Divide into pairs. Create two lines of masking tape on the floor about five feet (1.5 meters) apart. Each team's member should stand behind their line, facing the other team. One player should toss popcorn to her teammate (the lion). The "lion" should try to catch the popcorn in his mouth. When a "lion" catches a piece of popcorn, he should say, "My mouth is sealed shut." The first team to catch five pieces of popcorn in the "lion's" mouth wins.

Power Charge

Break into small groups and discuss the importance of remaining faithful to God. Remind children that sometimes having character can take courage. Ask children:

- What are some things that a person of character does?
- How can you respond to people who may challenge your faith?

Alternate Voltage

For added fun, increase the number of children throwing popcorn to each "lion."

Goldfish Toss

Starter

This game encourages children to obey God.

Read Jonah 1. Remind children that God had important work for Jonah.
He told Jonah to go to the city of Nineveh and tell the people that they needed to repent, turn from their evil ways, and follow Him. Unfortunately, when Jonah disobeyed God, he invited disaster into his life. Sitting inside a big fish, Jonah realized his mistake. Read Jonah 2:7–10, 3:10. Ask children:

- What was Jonah's mistake?

- Why is it important to obey God?

Introduce the game by saying, "Let's do to some goldfish what the big fish did to Jonah."

Power Tools

- Fish-shaped crackers
- Masking tape
- Measuring tape

Power Source

"But I, with a song of thanksgiving, will sacrifice to you. What I have vowed I will make good. Salvation comes from the Lord." Jonah 2:9

Bible Story Game

Explain that one at a time, the children should step up to a starting line (marked with masking tape) and toss a fish-shaped cracker as far as they can. Whoever tosses it the farthest wins. Use a measuring tape to track the results. Allow each player to have two or three turns.

Power Charge

At the end of class, pray with children that they will have the wisdom and strength to obey the Lord. Remind them that obedience to God means that they obey their parents and teachers. Then, give each child a small package of fish-shaped crackers as a reminder of the lesson.

Alternate Voltage

For an added challenge, create a target on the floor where greater distance equals more points. Add the points together after each player makes three tosses.

Baby Care Relay

Starter

This game teaches about Jesus' birth and humanity. The birth of God's Son was a blessed, holy event. It marked the beginning of the final stage in God's redemption of mankind. Though He was God's Son, Jesus was still a human with the same needs that we have.

God had a plan to redeem humanity. It was put in motion many centuries ago, and Jesus' birth marked the beginning of the final stage. Read Luke 2:1–14. Explain that today, you want to honor Jesus and His birth. It is important to acknowledge that He lived as we live. He walked, ate, slept, and experienced joy and sadness. He was God's Son, but He was still a man. Ask children:

- Who was Jesus?
- What did Jesus' birth mean?

Power Tools

- 10 large baby dolls
- 10 newborn diapers with reposition tape
- Masking tape

Power Source

"Today in the town of David a Savior has been born to you; he is Christ the Lord." Luke 2:11

Bible Story Game

Divide into two teams. First, demonstrate how to diaper a baby. Then, one at a time, have players race from the starting line (marked with masking tape) to the other end of the playing area where they should diaper a doll. Once they correctly diaper the doll, they should race back to the starting line and tag the next player in line. The first team to diaper all five of its dolls wins.

Power Charge

Break into small groups and discuss:

- Why did Jesus come to Earth?
- Why do you think He came as a baby?

Alternate Voltage

Ask if anyone would like to know Jesus as their personal savior. Lead them in the prayer of salvation.

Match the Stars

Energy Level Medium

Starter

This game tells the story of the Magi being led to Jesus, reminding children that God still leads us today.

Read Matthew 2:9–11. Talk about how God wanted the Magi to find Jesus so that they could worship Him, but they didn't know which way to go. He put a bright star in the sky to show them the way. Soon, they found out exactly where Jesus was.

• Why do you think God wanted the Magi to worship Jesus at His birth?

Power Tools

• Sheets of yellow construction paper, one per child
• Sheets of white construction paper, one per child
• Double-sided tape
• Stopwatch

Power Source

Your word is a lamp to my feet and a light for my path.
Psalm 119:105

Bible Story Game

Stack one yellow piece and one white piece of paper together. Cut out a star shape, making two identical stars (one white, one yellow) for each child. Shape each star pair slightly differently from other pairs by size or shape. Attach the yellow stars on a board or wall. Announce that when you say, "Go!" children should race to the board and stick the matching white stars to the yellow stars. The player with the fastest time wins.

Power Charge

Explain that God still leads us and guides us today. He may not use a bright star, but He uses His Word. (Read Psalm 119:105.) It leads us and guides us in all that we do. Break into small groups and discuss:

• What are some other ways that God leads us?
• How does God lead us through His Word?

Alternate Voltage

Use glow-in-the-dark paper or paint on the star shapes. When the children finish, dim the lights to see the stars glow.

Musical Chairs

Starter

Patience can be a difficult characteristic to develop, but it is important. This game reminds children that patience is a fruit of the Spirit, one of the attributes that lets others see the impact that Jesus has made in our lives.

Read Luke 2:22–35. Tell children that Simeon was a patient man. He patiently prayed for God to save Israel. Like Simeon, we don't always get what we want nor get it when we want it. Children will learn about an important character trait—patience.
Ask children:

- What is patience?
- How do we become more patient?

Power Tools

- Music CD
- CD player
- 1 less chair than the number of children

Power Source

. . . we pray this in order that you may live a life worthy of the Lord . . . being strengthened with all power according to his glorious might so that you may have great endurance and patience . . . .
Colossians 1:10–11

Bible Story Game

Remind children of the rules for Musical Chairs. Start the music and have players walk around the chairs. Periodically, stop the music. When the music stops, players should quickly find a seat. There should always be one less chair than the number of players. The player left standing is eliminated. Then, remove one chair and restart the game. Repeat the process until there is one player left.

Power Charge

Break into small groups and discuss:
- With whom do you need to be more patient this week?
- How can you be more patient toward that person?
- Why is it important to be patient with others?

Alternate Voltage

Use this game to introduce children to positive Christian music. Consider awarding the winner the music CD that you played during the game.

Just Like Us

Energy Level Medium

Starter

This game reminds children that Jesus was God, but He was also a man—and had to grow up just like any other boy.

Read Luke 2:52. Talk about how Jesus was fully God, but He was also fully man. He came to Earth so that He could live like a man and pay the price for our sins. He had to grow up just like we do—playing, learning, eating, and more. Ask children:

- What are some things Jesus might have done as a child?

Power Tools

- Masking tape
- Measuring tape

Power Source

. . . Jesus grew in wisdom and stature, and in favor with God and men. Luke 2:52

Bible Story Game

One by one, the children will compete in a standing distance jump. Beginning from the starting line (marked with masking tape), players should leap as far as they can. The player who jumps the farthest distance wins.

Power Charge

Jesus grew just like we do. His body grew from a small boy to a tall man. He grew smarter and stronger, and He grew to learn and love the Old Testament Scriptures. Break into small groups and discuss the different things that we can do today to grow stronger in God's Word just as young Jesus did.

Alternate Voltage

Instead of jumping for distance, have children jump for height.

 CD-204072 • *180 Faith-Charged Games* • © Carson-Dellosa

Scripture Races

Energy Level

Low

Starter

This game recalls Jesus at the Temple as a young boy, acknowledging that He was the Son of God—an important truth we all must believe for salvation.

Read Luke 2:41–52. Talk about how Joseph and Mary were traveling home when they realized Jesus was not with them. They quickly returned to Jerusalem and found Him three days later at the Temple. When Mary asked where He had been, Jesus replied that He was at His Father's house. This is the first time we see Jesus saying that He is God's Son. Ask children:

- Do you think Joseph and Mary understood at the time what Jesus was saying?

Power Tools

- Bible, one per child, preferably all in the same translation

Power Source

If anyone acknowledges that Jesus is the Son of God, God lives in him and he in God. 1 John 4:15

Bible Story Game

Explain that for this game, players should race against each other to look up Scriptures that you call out by book, chapter, and verse. The first player to find each Scripture should read it to the group. The child who finds the most Scriptures first wins. If a player finds five Scriptures first, he can be declared the winner and sit out while the others compete. (See suggested Scriptures on page 190.)

Power Charge

Explain that all of these Scriptures have one thing in common: they talk about Jesus being God's Son. Break into small groups and discuss:

- What evidence was there that Jesus was God's Son?

Alternate Voltage

If you regularly encourage children to bring their Bibles, have them use their own Bibles for this game. Have children with Bibles share with those who do not. Students sharing a Bible can take turns finding the verses and reading.

Keep Your Focus

Starter

This game focuses on how John the Baptist stayed true to his calling, despite criticism, and eventually baptized Jesus.

Read Matthew 3:1–17. Talk about how John the Baptist knew that Jesus was coming, and let everyone know it. Some religious and political leaders did not like John. It probably didn't help that he lived in the desert and ate grasshoppers and honey! But John stayed focused on what he knew was the truth. Ask children:

- Do you think it was hard for John the Baptist to remain focused on his calling?

- Do you think he ever thought about giving up?

Power Tools

- 2 spoons
- 2 table-tennis balls
- Masking tape

Power Source

Run in such a way as to get the prize. 1 Corinthians 9:24

Bible Story Game

Divide into two teams. One player on each team should takes a turn putting a table-tennis ball on a spoon and carrying it from the starting line (marked with masking tape) to the far side of the room and back without letting the ball drop. If the ball falls, the player should start over before tagging the next team member. The team who completes the course first wins.

Power Charge

Explain that John the Baptist had many opportunities to quit—but he didn't! He kept his focus on what God called him to do—tell others about Jesus. It may not have been easy, but in the end, he received the high honor of baptizing Jesus. Break into small groups and discuss:

- What is something you know God wants you to do that is pretty difficult?

- What can you do to keep focused on doing what's right?

Alternate Voltage

Instead of using table-tennis balls, use plastic grasshoppers to tie in with the lesson, or cotton balls to make the game more challenging.

Temptation Topple

Energy Level
Low

Starter

Temptation is all around us. Satan uses worldly things to gain a place in our hearts. Today, children learn that even Jesus was tempted. He didn't give into temptation, and neither should they.

Explain that Satan wants to pull us away from God. He does this by tempting us to do things that are wrong. Read Matthew 4:1–11. Ask children:

- How does Satan try to tempt us?
- Does he use big temptations or little ones?

Power Tools

- Wooden craft sticks

Power Source

The thief comes only to steal and kill and destroy; I have come that they may have life, and have it to the full. John 10:10

Bible Story Game

Build a tower with the craft sticks. Allow children to take turns removing a craft stick until the tower falls. The player who makes the tower fall rebuilds it so children can play again.

Power Charge

Ask children:

- Did the tower fall because of one big move or did it fall because the structure was weakened?

Explain to children that Satan operates the same way. Instead of one big move, he usually attempts to weaken us with little moves over time.

Alternate Voltage

Read the following Scriptures aloud and discuss them. Give children reminder notes with the Scriptures on them. Then, ask children to memorize them by the following week. Reward those who do this.

- Romans 8:15
- Acts 17:28
- 1 John 3:1
- 1 John 4:4

Answering the Call

Energy Level High

Starter

When Jesus called the first disciples to join Him, it was only the beginning. This game will remind children that they're called to follow Jesus too.

Read Matthew 4:18–22. Explain to children that Jesus had helpers, people He trusted to help Him fulfill His life's purpose. Ask children:

- What does it mean to be a disciple?
- How can we follow Jesus today?

Power Tools

- 3–5 cell phones

Power Source

"Come, follow me," Jesus said, "and I will make you fishers of men." Matthew 4:19

Bible Story Game

Hide the cell phones around the room before the children arrive. Divide into two teams. Make sure that all of their ringers are set to the loudest ring tone. When the game begins, call the phones one at a time. Players should search to find the cell phones. The team who finds the most cell phones wins.

Power Charge

Talk to children about the different kinds of "calls" they may receive from God. Here are some suggestions for calls from God:

- Be a friend to someone whom others don't like.
- Share Jesus with someone who doesn't know Him.
- Become a pastor or a missionary.
- Give some of your toys to someone who doesn't have any.

Alternate Voltage

For extra fun, change the phones' ringers to funny sounds or songs that children can identify.

Parachute Pick-Up

Starter

This game recalls the Sermon on the Mount where Jesus taught the Beatitudes. Use this game to remind children that they are in charge of their attitudes.

Read Matthew 5:1–12. These words of Jesus are often called the Beatitudes. *Beatitude* means "happy" or "blissful." The Beatitudes show us that having the right attitude about life will help us to live joyful lives and be a blessing to others. Ask children:

- Why do you think Jesus made a point of talking about attitudes?

Power Tools

- Numbered table-tennis balls, one per child
- Bedsheet

Power Source

So then, let us not be like others, who are asleep, but let us be alert and self-controlled.
1 Thessalonians 5:6

Bible Story Game

Assign each child a number. Give each child a numbered ball. Have the players scatter around the edges of the bedsheet and pick it up. When you say, "Go!" the children should throw their balls onto the sheet. Using their grip on the sheet, the players should try to throw off other balls while protecting their own. Remind children not to be too rough. As balls are tossed off of the sheet, call out the numbers. It takes a lot of control to use this strategy. The player with the remaining table-tennis ball wins.

Power Charge

Explain that some people think that they can't control their attitudes. They think they were just made one way or another. But God disagrees. He says we can control our attitudes, and we must if we want to live a happy and enjoyable life. Ask children:

- Which attitudes do you think are the hardest to control?
- How does controlling your attitude make your life more enjoyable?

Alternate Voltage

For a fun warm-weather activity, use water balloons. Those that fall off but don't pop can be returned to the bedsheet.

Aim for God

Starter

This game reinforces the lesson of seeking God and aiming for His kingdom and His righteousness before other goals.

Read Matthew 6:25–34. Talk about how God doesn't want us to worry about what could happen. He wants us to look only to Him, trusting Him to take care of us, just like He does the birds and flowers. Ask children:

• What kinds of things do you worry about?

Power Tools

• Masking tape
• 8–10 beanbags or sock balls

Power Source

. . . seek first his kingdom and his righteousness, and all these things will be given to you as well. Matthew 6:33

Bible Story Game

Divide into two teams. Create a target on the ground with masking tape. Give each team an equal number of beanbags. Tell players that each beanbag represents a worry discussed above. Players attempt to get their beanbags as close to the bull's-eye as possible. Hits closest to the bull's-eye score highest. The team with the higher score wins.

Power Charge

Explain that when we seek God first, not only can we count on Him to take care of us, but we will also be given more than enough. Break into small groups and discuss:

• When was a time you know that God provided for you or someone you love?

• What is something you're going to stop worrying about and trust God with?

Alternate Voltage

As an alternate game, use magnetic darts and a dartboard.

The Squeeze

Energy Level Medium

Starter

Tell students that they will see how they "measure up" today. Read John 2:1–11. Tell children that this is the first miracle Jesus performed, and it reminds us that Jesus changes lives. Just as He changed the water into wine, He can change us too. Ask children:

- How did Jesus change lives in the Bible?

- How does Jesus change lives today?

Power Tools

- 20 lemons, halved

- 2 measuring bowls

- 2 juicers

Power Source

Therefore, if anyone is in Christ, he is a new creation; the old has gone, the new has come!
2 Corinthians 5:17

Bible Story Game

Divide into two teams. Have team members take turns squeezing juice from lemons for three minutes. To determine the winning team, compare the measurements of juice contained in the bowls. The team with the most juice wins.

Power Charge

Make lemonade for the children. Remind them that only Jesus can quench our thirst for peace, happiness, and fulfillment.

Alternate Voltage

Allow children to sample the unsweetened juice and sweetened lemonade. Then, compare it to the difference between the old and new creation.

Ring String

Energy Level Low

Starter

Today's game teaches children about the fruit of the Spirit—love, joy, peace, patience, kindness, goodness, faithfulness, gentleness, and self-control. Explain that we should exhibit these qualities to those around us so that they will know that we are followers of Christ.

Read Luke 6:43–45. Let children know that God's Word tells us to have the fruit of the Spirit in our lives. Having this fruit is called godly character. When we exhibit these traits to others, we show the world that God has made a difference in us. Ask children:

- What is the fruit of our lives?
- What is godly character?

Power Tools

- Fruit-flavored ring cereal
- Lengths of string, approximately 16–20", each with one end tied in a large knot, one per child
- Stopwatch

Power Source

"Each tree is recognized by its own fruit." Luke 6:44

Bible Story Game

Assign "fruit of the Spirit" names (love, joy, peace, etc.) to the colors present in your cereal mixture. Give players two minutes to string together as many cereal rings as possible. The player to string the most cereal rings wins. Allow children to wear their completed strings as necklaces.

Power Charge

Discuss each of the fruit of the Spirit so that children understand what each means. Give examples of each. Give children the color key from the game so that they can explain the fruit of the spirit to their parents using their necklaces.

Alternate Voltage

For a fun, tangible reminder of God's fruit, create a fruit buffet for children to sample at the end of class. Explain that just as we can combine physical fruit to make fruit salad or fruit kabobs, God combines spiritual fruit in perfect combinations to bless others and draw them to Him.

Vacuum Races

Energy
Level
High

Starter

This game reminds children that Jesus forgives sin. Just as Jesus removed the sin in the related Bible story, He will remove it from our lives so that we can live a clean life for Him.

Read Luke 7:36–50. Remind children that the woman in the story was considered unclean. Others thought she was a lost cause, but not Jesus. Ask children:

- Why did Jesus forgive this woman's sins?
- If we need forgiveness for our sins, what should we do?

Power Tools

- 2 cordless hand vacuums
- Confetti
- Masking tape

Power Source

"Your sins are forgiven." Luke 7:48

Bible Story Game

Divide into two teams, and have children line up behind two starting lines (marked by masking tape). Sprinkle an equal, small amount of confetti in two areas on the floor. The first player in line holds the vacuum and at the signal to start, the first player from each team vacuums up all of his confetti. Sprinkle new confetti after each player. The first team to vacuum up all of its confetti wins.

Power Charge

Break into small groups and discuss:

- Did anyone leave a trace of confetti on the floor?
- When God cleanses us from our sins, does He still see even a trace of sin in us?
- How does it feel to know that you are forgiven—that your sins have been washed "as white as snow"?

Alternate Voltage

If only one vacuum is available, allow players to complete the task one after the other, and time each player with a stopwatch.

Hard-Boiled Egg Spin

Energy Level Low

Starter

This game reassures children that even when problems seem to spin out of control (schoolwork is hard, friends turn against us, or parents divorce), Jesus can still bring peace.

Read Matthew 8:23–27. Explain to children that the disciples were facing a very scary situation. At any moment, their boat could have sunk, but Jesus came through for them. Ask children:

- When difficulties arise, how should we respond?
- Who can we turn to for peace?

Power Tools

- Hard-boiled eggs, one per child
- Bell
- Table

Power Source

"The Lord turn His face toward you and give you peace." Numbers 6:26

Bible Story Game

Explain that at the sound of a starting bell, the players spin their eggs as fast as they can. Pass out the eggs. The player whose egg spins the longest wins. If an egg falls off of the table, it is out of play.

Power Charge

Jesus' presence in our lives gives us peace—not only the peace of knowing that we're going to Heaven, but peace for right now. When things spin out of control in our lives, we need to turn to Jesus. Break into small groups and discuss:

- Have you ever felt like you were spinning out of control? Did you ask God for peace?
- How did He respond?

Alternate Voltage

If a large table is not available, have children spin the eggs on the floor.

Saltine Houses

Energy Level Low

Starter

This game retells Jesus' parable of the man who built his house on the rock and reminds children that putting God's Word into practice creates a sure foundation in their lives.

Read Matthew 7:24–27. Talk about Jesus' parable of building a house on rock versus building a house on sand. The house on the rock is the only one that will remain standing when a storm hits. Ask children:

- What does the rain and wind in this parable represent?

Power Tools

- Box of square saltine crackers

Power Source

"Everyone who hears these words of mine and puts them into practice is like a wise man who built his house on the rock." Matthew 7:24

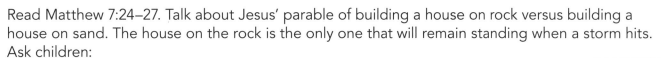

Bible Story Game

One by one, have players use saltine crackers to build a house (like a house of cards). If their house falls, they get credit for any story with at least two "walls." Whoever builds the house with the most stories wins.

Power Charge

Explain that God wants our lives to be strong. He doesn't want the troubles of life to push us over. The only way to have a strong life is to hear God's Word and put it into practice. Break into small groups and discuss:

- How can we regularly hear God's Word?
- How can we regularly put His Word into practice?

Alternate Voltage

For younger children, change the game so that they stack crackers flat on top of each other.

Help Your Neighbor

Energy Level Medium

Starter

This game tells the story of the Good Samaritan, reminding children that God wants us to show compassion to all those around us.

Read Luke 10:25–37. Let children know that we have neighbors all around us. Whether we're at school, at home, at church, or on sports teams, there are other people—children your age—who need to see God's love from us. Ask children:

• What was the purpose of this parable?

• What did Jesus mean when he asked who was a "neighbor" in this story?

Power Tools

• 10 scarves

• 10 chairs

Power Source

Love your neighbor as yourself. Luke 10:27

Bible Story Game

Tie five scarves to the legs or bottoms of the chairs for each team. Divide into two teams. Make sure that the scarves cannot be removed easily and are placed as inconspicuously as possible. Instruct teams to work together to remove the scarves from the chairs. The first team to remove all five scarves wins.

Power Charge

Showing compassion to others and helping those in need is a great way to show God's love to people who are hurting. Ask children:

• Did you have to help one another to remove the scarves?

• Why is it important to help others?

Alternate Voltage

Have children commit to helping one person this week. Pass out paper and pens so that children can write the name of the person they will help. Then, instruct them to place this paper somewhere prominent (the bathroom mirror, the refrigerator, their dresser, etc.). Be sure to ask them about it next week.

Bandage Tag

Starter

This game reminds children that Jesus healed those who came to Him—and He still heals today through miracles and His Word.

Read Matthew 12:15, Luke 4:18, and John 6:63. Tell children that when Jesus was on Earth, He healed everyone who came to Him. He turned no one away. He healed through touch and through His Word. Ask children:

- Does Jesus still heal today?

- Can you think of someone you know who has been healed?

Power Tools

- None

Power Source

Many followed Him, and He healed all their sick. Matthew 12:15

Bible Story Game

Take children outside or to a large, open indoor space. Ask for a volunteer to be "it." That player should chase the others until she tags one on the arm or leg. When a player is tagged, he becomes the new "it." He must hold the spot where he was tagged, pretending to hold onto a bandage while he tries to tag another player.

Power Charge

Explain that Jesus still heals people through miracles and through His Word. He will help doctors when they perform operations. Jesus helps us keep going and helps us heal. Have children break into small groups and pray for healing for those who need it.

Alternate Voltage

Ask someone who has experienced God's healing, whether through a miracle or a doctor's care, to share his story.

Loaf Pass

Energy Level **Medium**

Starter

This game will help remind children that the Lord provides for His people.

Read Matthew 14:13–21. Explain to children that people were hungry—spiritually hungry—for the truth that Jesus taught them. That's why they followed Him wherever He went. On this day, Jesus fed more than 5,000 people with only five loaves of bread and two fish—truly a miracle. Ask children:

- What does this miracle show about Jesus?
- How does it apply to us today?

Power Tools

- 2 loaves of French bread
- Bell

Power Source

He has shown kindness by giving you rain from heaven and crops in their seasons; He provides you with plenty of food and fills your hearts with joy. Acts 14:17

Bible Story Game

Divide into two equal teams. Explain that at the sound of the starting bell, players should pass the bread from person to person. Each teammate should tear off a small piece of bread. Players continue to pass the bread until every player on the team has taken some. The challenge is to make sure that everyone gets some bread. Whichever team passes their bread first and has enough for everyone wins.

Power Charge

Just as Jesus provided for the 5,000 people, He continues to provide for us today. Break into small groups and discuss:

- How does God provide for your needs today?

Alternate Voltage

To make the game even more challenging, pass a hamburger bun.

Personal Thanks

Energy Level
Low

Starter

This game recalls one of 10 lepers who Jesus healed and returned to thank Him.

Read Luke 17:12–19. Talk about how Jesus met 10 people with leprosy and healed them. Sadly, only one of the 10 returned to say "Thank you!" Ask children:

- Would you have gone back to thank Jesus? Why?

- Why do you think the others didn't return?

Power Tools

- None

Power Source

Give thanks to the Lord, call on His name; make known among the nations what He has done. Psalm 105:1

Bible Story Game

Starting at the front of the room, ask each child to give thanks for something that begins with the same letter as the first letter of his name. For example, a child named Henry might give thanks for his house. This game often becomes funny. More importantly, it causes children to reflect on the things that they are thankful for.

Power Charge

Explain that God is always worthy of our thanks—whether it's a little thing like a meal or a big thing like a miracle. Break into small groups and discuss:

- What are some things that you thank God for every day?

- When is a good time to give thanks?

Alternate Voltage

After each child says what she is thankful for, have the group repeat it in a sentence using the child's name, such as "Jen is thankful for juice."

Grab the Blessing

Energy Level **High**

Starter

This game tells the story of Jesus blessing the children, reminding children that they can approach God eagerly.

Read Luke 18:15–17. Talk about how children were approaching Jesus, and He was blessing them. When the disciples saw the children coming to Jesus, they tried to stop them; they didn't want Jesus to be bothered by the children. But Jesus said that everyone should come to Him the way the children did! Ask children:

- What do you think Jesus liked best about the way that the children came to Him?

Power Tools

- 20 balls of various sizes
- Star sticker
- Bell

Power Source

"Let the little children come to me." Luke 18:16

Bible Story Game

Place the star sticker on one ball. Then, place the balls around the room. Explain that at the sound of the bell, players should race around the room looking for the ball with the star sticker on it. The player who finds it wins.

Power Charge

Explain that God doesn't want us to feel uncomfortable coming to Him. He wants us to approach Him eagerly—with the same anticipation and excitement that they showed when they were playing the game. Ask children:

- What are some ways that you approach God?
- Why do you think God wants us to approach Him eagerly?

Alternate Voltage

Add more balls to make the game even more challenging. Use a variety of balls: baseballs, basketballs, soccer balls, table-tennis balls, bowling balls, exercise balls, golf balls, etc.

Penny Pop Relay

Energy Level High

Starter

God wants us to be cheerful givers. He doesn't want us to be stingy. This game can help to teach children the right way to give—with humility, remembering that all we have belongs to God.

Read Mark 12:41–44. Explain that giving is an important form of worship. It is a way to show that we serve God.

Ask children:

- What was so different about this widow's giving?

- What should we learn from her example?

Power Tools

- Balloons, one per child
- 2 pennies per child
- 2 chairs
- 2 bowls
- Masking tape

Power Source

Each man should give what he has decided in his heart to give, not reluctantly or under compulsion, for God loves a cheerful giver.
2 Corinthians 9:7

Bible Story Game

Divide into two teams. Give each player a balloon containing two pennies inside. At the signal to start, one player from each team should race from the starting line (marked with masking tape) across the playing area to a chair. He will pop his balloon by sitting on it. Then, he will retrieve the two pennies that were inside the balloon and race back to the starting line where he will deposit his pennies in the bowl. The first team to complete this wins.

Power Charge

Discuss with children where their church offerings go. Explain that it goes to pay for supplies for the service and the church's expenses. Give them an opportunity to see how the money is used so that they can understand the part that their giving plays in the life of the church.

Alternate Voltage

Use this lesson to start an outreach. Here are some ideas:

- Raise money to support a foreign missionary (Make sure children know who this person is and what the person is doing.)
- Collect clothing for a needy child
- Food drive for a local charity—a homeless shelter, food bank, children's home, or a family in need

Sharing the Gospel

Energy Level
Low

Starter

This game provides a great opportunity to teach children about sharing the gospel. It is a chance for them to begin fulfilling the Great Commission in their own lives.

Three days after Jesus died on the cross, He returned to Earth and gave His disciples an important message. Read Mark 16:15–18. That message applies to us today. Ask children:

- What did Jesus mean when He said, "Go into all the world"?
- What are our worlds?

Power Tools

- None

Power Source

"Go into all the world and preach the good news to all creation." Mark 16:15

Bible Story Game

Divide into pairs. Have children role-play situations in which they can share Jesus, such as leading someone in the prayer of salvation, inviting someone to church, or sharing a testimony. Have each pair perform its skit for the class.

Power Charge

Make sure that children understand the "good news" in the Power Source verse. Have each child think of at least one person they know with whom they can share the good news of Jesus. Explain that sharing Jesus isn't about a formula; it's about letting their lives, words, and actions show just what their Savior means to them.

Alternate Voltage

In order to help children share Jesus, plan a special *Invite My Friends to Church Day*. Make this day special by planning a "good news" service, complete with "good news" message, special activities, and possibly a cookout. This could even be a great outreach for the entire church.

Prayer Shuffle

Energy Level Low

Starter

This game will teach children that prayer is an important part of a Christian's life. Thankfully, God is never too tired, too busy, or too far away to hear what concerns us.

Read Matthew 6:5–15. Explain to children that when you pray, you are talking to God, the Creator of the universe. Prayer involves talking to God, acknowledging His greatness, sharing your concerns, and asking for direction. Ask children:

- Why is it important to pray?
- Do you ever wonder what to pray about?

Power Tools

- 2 sets of index cards, each with a portion of the Lord's Prayer printed on each (See example on page 190.)

Power Source

The Lord is far from the wicked but he hears the prayer of the righteous. Proverbs 15:29

Bible Story Game

Write the Lord's Prayer on a board and allow the children to review it. Divide into two teams. Place the cards facedown in front of the first player on each team. On your signal, the players should turn over the cards and place them in order. When one player finishes, he shuffles the cards. Then, the next player on the team takes a turn. The first team to have all players put the cards in order wins.

Power Charge

Break into small groups and take prayer requests. Give each child the opportunity to pray (if they choose to). Let this exercise encourage children to pray aloud for one other.

Alternate Voltage

Instead of having children arrange the cards on a flat surface, have them tape the cards in order on a wall so that the entire group can watch their progress.

May I?

Energy
Level
Medium

Starter

This game is a reminder of the free gift of salvation. More than anything, God wants to give us eternity with Him. All we have to do is ask.

Read Matthew 7:7–12. Talk about the things that God has given each of us. Then explain that although all of those things are good gifts, the greatest thing that God wants to give us is salvation. We only have to ask Him for it by surrendering our lives to Him. Ask children:

- What are some things that God has given you?

- Why is salvation so important?

- How do we ask God for it?

Power Tools

- Masking tape

Power Source

"Ask and it will be given to you; seek and you will find; knock and the door will be opened to you." Matthew 7:7

Bible Story Game

Create a list of commands before the game. (See page 190 for examples.) Explain to children that they will be playing a variation of Mother, May I. Instead of asking, "Mother, may I?" after each command, they should ask, "Pastor, may I?" or "Teacher, may I?"

Children should line up at the starting line (marked with masking tape) at the front of the room. One at a time, ask children to accomplish one command. With each command, players must ask, "Pastor, may I?" before doing it. If they forget, they should take two steps backward. For each command that they complete correctly, they should hop forward once. The first player to reach the finish line wins.

Power Charge

Sing a salvation-themed Christian children's song together, such as "Do Lord (Way Beyond the Blue"). You can look up the lyrics online if you don't know them.

Alternate Voltage

For extra fun, do all of the steps and hops backward.

Climbing for Jesus

Starter

This game recalls how Jesus befriended a despised tax collector, Zacchaeus.

Read Luke 19:1–10. Talk about how Zacchaeus really wanted to see Jesus. Because he was short, he ran ahead of the crowd and climbed a tree in order to see Jesus. Jesus called Zacchaeus by name and stayed at his house. This made a lot of people angry because they felt that Zacchaeus did bad things. But Jesus corrected them, stating that Zacchaeus was exactly the kind of person He came to Earth to save. Ask children:

- What did Jesus mean when He said that He came to save the lost?

Power Tools

- Jungle gym or any type of climbing apparatus

Power Source

"For the Son of Man came to seek and to save what was lost." Luke 19:10

Bible Story Game

Have children take turns dramatizing being Zacchaeus, the crowd, and Jesus walking by. Let anyone who would like to be Zacchaeus climb onto the jungle gym to serve as the tree.

Power Charge

Explain that God loves it when we live good lives, but He also understands when we mess up. Some people mess up very badly. That doesn't scare God away. He wants to help everyone. Break into small groups and discuss:

- How do you think Jesus wants you to treat people who mess up?

Alternate Voltage

Use a stopwatch to time individual players for the best racing time.

7-13-15

Popcorn Pop

Energy Level High

Starter

This game reminds children of Nicodemus, who visited Jesus at night, to find out how he could get to Heaven.

Read John 3:1–21. Discuss Jesus' answer to Nicodemus: the only way to get to Heaven is to be born again. That is, you have to make Jesus your Lord and start a new life in Him. Jesus meant that you must be born as God's son or daughter. Ask children:

- Why do you think Jesus called becoming a Christian being "born again"?

Power Tools

- Lots of popcorn in a large bucket (about 6 large bags)
- 2 flexible paper plates
- 2 large bowls

Power Source

Jesus declared, "I tell you the truth, no one can see the kingdom of God unless he is born again." John 3:3

Bible Story Game

Divide into two teams. Explain that when you say, "Go!" one player from each team should get a large scoop of popcorn on her plate from the bucket. Then, she should hop across the room on one foot and dump the remaining popcorn on her plate into a bowl. She should return to the start. The next person should take a turn. After one team completes the race, the game is over and the bowls are compared. The team whose bowl has more popcorn wins.

Power Charge

Show an unpopped kernel and a piece of popped corn to children. Tell them that being born is like the unpopped kernel and being born again is like the popped corn. The popping corn can reach its full potential when it is fully popped. We reach our full potential when we are born again. Give each child some popcorn to take home.

Alternate Voltage

Have children spin or complete other movements to make the game more challenging.

Race to Jesus

Energy Level High

Starter

This game reminds children of the faith of the four men who carried their paralyzed friend to Jesus for healing.

Explain that Jesus healed multitudes of people when He was on Earth. He did it to show God's love for people. Read Mark 2:1–12. Ask children:

- What does it mean when the Bible says, "Jesus saw their faith"?

- How was the man healed? Was he healed in his body or in his spirit?

Power Tools

- Twin-sized flat sheet
- Large doll
- Chairs or cones
- Stopwatch
- Masking tape

Power Source

[Jesus] said to the paralytic, "I tell you, get up, take your mat and go home." Mark 2:10–11

Bible Story Game

Using chairs or cones, create an obstacle course around the room so that teams must maneuver around and over items. Divide into teams of four players. Each team member should hold a corner of a sheet with a large doll in the center. Explain that at the starting signal, each team should cross the starting line (marked with masking tape) and move through the obstacle course. Use a stopwatch to determine which team completes the course in the shortest amount of time.

Power Charge

Take prayer requests for healing. If possible, have a leader write or type these requests on paper and make enough copies so that each child can take a list home and pray for those people. Be sure to ask for praise reports over the next several weeks.

Alternate Voltage

Encourage teams to work together and move slowly. If a team drops the doll, they should start over.

Lazarus Wrap

Energy Level
Medium

Starter

In this game, children learn about Lazarus and are encouraged to give thanks for the new spiritual life that Jesus has given to each of us.

Read John 11:17–44. When Jesus raised Lazarus from the dead, He restored his physical body and gave him new life. As God's children, we have also been given a new life—not only a new spirit, but eternal life with Jesus. Ask children:

- How have we been raised from the dead?
- What has changed in our lives because we have a new Spirit?

Power Tools

- Two rolls of bath tissue
- Masking tape

Power Source

"I am the resurrection and the life. He who believes in me will live, even though he dies; and whoever lives and believes in me will never die." John 11:25–26

Bible Story Game

Divide into two teams. Mark a finish line at one end of the room with masking tape. Gather each team in a tight group. Select a volunteer from each team to be the "wrapper." The "wrapper" should wrap his team with bath tissue. (Tell the children to remain still to avoid tearing the tissue.) After each team is wrapped, they should walk slowly to the finish line without tearing the tissue. If they tear the tissue, they should return to the starting line and begin again. After each team crosses the finish line, they can break the tissue and place it in the trash.

Power Charge

Read the Power Source verse aloud. Ask children:

- What did it feel like to be bound, unable to move?
- How did it feel to break free from the bandages and throw them away?

Remind children that when we ask Jesus to come into our lives, we can shed the bindings around our hearts and lives that have kept us from truly living and feeling joy. Jesus gives us a new spirit, a new life, and a new hope of eternal life with Him in Heaven.

Alternate Voltage

Take testimonies from children and adults, sharing the difference that being a Christian has made in their lives.

Jerusalem Limbo

Energy Level High

Starter

This game reminds children of Jesus entering Jerusalem and that God deserves all of our praise.

Read Luke 19:29–40. When Jesus entered Jerusalem riding on a donkey, the people celebrated and shouted their praise, giving glory to God. Giving glory means giving someone your highest honor. Ask children:

- Why do you think people gave God glory when they saw Jesus?

Power Tools

- Broomstick
- CD Player
- Praise and worship CD

Power Source

"You are worthy, our Lord and God, to receive glory and honor and power, for you created all things, and by your will they were created and have their being."
Revelation 4:11

Bible Story Game

Play upbeat praise and worship music. Have two adults hold the broomstick as the players take turns walking under the broomstick, bending backward to limbo. If a player touches the stick with her body or touches the ground with her hands, she is out. Each round, the broomstick should be lowered by an inch. After each child passes under the broomstick, have him shout a reason to praise God! The last player limboing wins!

Power Charge

Explain that God deserves all of our praise and worship. There is no one higher than He is. Discuss the following with the group:

- What are some reasons God deserves our praise?
- What is something God has recently done that you can praise Him for?

Lead the children in a praise and worship celebration to God.

Alternate Voltage

To reiterate the message of Jesus' entry into Jerusalem, use Israeli or Messianic Jewish music.

Fishing for Clips

Starter

In this game, children recall the story of Peter and the fish, reminding them that God is our provider and that we can turn to Him when in need.

Read Matthew 17:24–27. Reaffirm to children that God loves us and that we can trust Him to help us when we have a need.

Ask children:

- How did Jesus instruct Peter to pay the Temple tax?
- What does this story show us about Jesus?

Power Tools

- Two makeshift fishing poles (stick or broom handle with a string and magnet attached)
- Large box of metal paper clips
- Stopwatch

Power Source

"Cast your cares on the Lord and he will sustain you; he will never let the righteous fall." Psalm 55:22

Bible Story Game

Divide into two teams. Scatter the paper clips on the floor. Each player should have one minute to fish for as many paper clips as possible. The team to catch the most paper clips wins.

Power Charge

Read the Power Source verse aloud. Remind children that because God cares for us, He will provide for us—sometimes in the most unexpected places and unexpected times! Ask children to testify of God's provision in their lives. Then, give each child an index card and a pen. Have each child write something that concerns her. Pray over the concerns as a group. Instruct children to take their cards home and pray over their concerns each day. Tell them that you want to hear when their prayer requests are answered. Follow up with children in the coming weeks.

Alternate Voltage

Write each word from the Power Source verse on a paper fish shape. Attach a paper clip to each fish. Have children catch the fish and put the verse in order.

Hot Potato Ball

Energy Level Medium

Starter

This passing game reminds children of the parable of the unmerciful servant, and how it is important to pass on to others the forgiveness that we received from Jesus.

Read Matthew 18:23–35. Encourage children that just as God displayed mercy and forgiveness to us, we should follow Jesus' example. Ask children:

- Why is it so important to show mercy and forgiveness to others?
- How did God show mercy to us?

Power Tools

- Ball
- Music CD
- CD player

Power Source

"Bear with each other and forgive whatever grievances you may have against one another. Forgive as the Lord forgave you." Colossians 3:13

Bible Story Game

Have children sit in a circle. Explain that at the start of the music, they should pass the ball around the circle. Each time they pass, they should pause to say, "Pass on the forgiveness." When the music stops, the player holding the ball is eliminated and should leave the circle. Continue the game until only the winning player remains.

Power Charge

Talk to the children about what forgiveness means.

- How does it feel when someone you love forgives you of something?
- How do you feel when you forgive someone else?

Ask if anyone needs to pass the forgiveness they have received from God on to someone else. Lead children in a prayer of forgiveness.

Alternate Voltage

Be sensitive to the fact that some children may be dealing with deep wounds. If any children need extra attention, have leaders ready to take them aside to pray and talk with them.

Penny Relay

Energy Level High

Starter

This game recalls the story of Jesus clearing the Temple, showing that God wants us to be respectful in His house.

Read Mark 11:15–19. Discuss how Jesus entered the Temple and saw something that angered Him: God's people had turned the Temple into a noisy marketplace. Immediately, He began to throw out everyone who was buying and selling there. Ask children:

- Why do you think Jesus behaved this way?
- How does Jesus want people to behave in church?

Power Tools

- Pennies, one per child
- 2 large bowls

Power Source

"Is it not written: 'My house will be called a house of prayer for all nations'? But you have made it 'a den of robbers.'" Mark 11:17

Bible Story Game

Divide into two teams. Place one bowl several feet away (1–2 meters) in front of each team. Give each child one penny. Explain that the first player in each team should balance the penny on her nose, carefully race to the bowl, and drop the penny into the bowl. If the penny falls, she should start over. When the penny is in the bowl, she should run back and tag the next player. The first team to drop all of their pennies in their bowl wins.

Power Charge

God's house, the church, is a place we go to worship Him. Jesus was angry because the people were not treating the Temple with respect and as a "house of prayer" as God intended. They were not only buying and selling items, but many were cheating the people out of money. Break into small groups and discuss.

- What are some ways we can respect God's house?

Alternate Voltage

Explain that there were many crowds in the Temple the day that Jesus was angered—people were buying or selling goods. To make the relay more challenging, have each team stand in a single file line a few feet apart. Each player should weave in and out of his team's line as he races to put his penny in the bowl.

A Humble Fit

Energy Level High

Starter

This game demonstrates the value of humility.

Read John 13:3–9, 12–17. Explain that in biblical times, people's feet got dirty from walking along dusty roads. A servant usually washed the feet of guests when they arrived at someone's home. When Jesus was celebrating Passover with His disciples, He used this opportunity to kneel before them and wash their feet. Peter had a hard time with this because he saw Jesus as his Lord—not his servant. Ask children:

- Why do you think Jesus washed the disciples' feet?
- How do you think the disciples felt when Jesus washed their feet?

Power Tools

- None

Power Source

"For whoever exalts himself will be humbled, and whoever humbles himself will be exalted." Matthew 23:12

Bible Story Game

Divide into two teams. Have the children remove their shoes and place them in a pile at one end of the room. Have the children sound off with a number from one to three on each team. Explain that when you say a number, everyone with that number should run and retrieve a shoe from the pile. The shoe should not be her own. The player should find a teammate's shoes! When she finds a teammate's show, she should race back to her team, kneel, and put the shoe on her teammate's foot. Then, the next player continues. If a player brings back a shoe that does not belong to his team, he should return it and he loses his turn. The first team to be wearing their shoes wins!

Power Charge

Explain that Jesus wanted to set an example for His disciples. He wanted them to realize that no one was greater than any other. So, He humbly washed their feet and told them to do the same for each other in the future—to live lives of humility and to serve each other. Break into small groups and discuss:

- What are some ways that you can live with humility?
- How does a person act if they aren't humble?

Alternate Voltage

Add extra shoes to the pile (that don't belong to anyone) to increase the challenge!

Hidden Treasure

Energy Level
Low

Starter

This game encourages children to use the gifts and talents that God has given them to help others and to share God's love.

Read Matthew 25:14–30. Give children examples of talents, such as playing an instrument, building things, creating art, cooking, excelling at math, etc. Encourage children to use their special gifts to serve God. Ask children:

- What are some gifts or talents that God has given us?

- How can we use these gifts or talents to help others?

Power Tools

- Chalkboard or whiteboard
- Chalk or marker

Power Source

"Well done, good and faithful servant! You have been faithful with a few things; I will put you in charge of many things."
Matthew 25:21

Bible Story Game

The object of the game is to guess each child's gift. Children can ask only questions that can be answered with *yes* or *no*. Each team begins with 1,000 points. Each time that the answer is *no*, deduct 100 points. Divide into two groups. Ask a volunteer to think about his specific gift. The team that correctly guesses the gift (and has the most points) wins.

Power Charge

Everyone has talents from God that should be used for His glory. God needs us to be willing to use our talents to serve Him and to share His love with others. Break into groups and discuss:

- What are your talents?
- How can you use them for God?

Some children may not think that they have any special talents. Take this opportunity to point out at least one talent for each child. Explain ways that God could use that gift.

Alternate Voltage

To earn bonus points, have the children share how the gift could be used to serve God.

The Helping Game

Energy Level Medium

Starter

This game reminds children that God wants us to show compassion toward others, especially those who are less fortunate.

Read Matthew 25:31–46. Explain to the children that showing compassion by helping others is a great way to share Jesus' love. Ask children:

- In this passage, what was the difference between the goats and the sheep?
- How does that apply to our lives?

Power Tools

- Small unbreakable objects (such as blocks, paperback books, coins, etc.), one per child
- Music CD
- CD Player

Power Source

"Whatever you did for one of the least of these brothers of mine, you did for me." Matthew 25:40

Bible Story Game

Give each child a small object. As the music plays, she should balance the object on her head while walking. If the object falls, she cannot catch it, but should freeze in place. The frozen player is "helpless" until someone places the object on her head. The frozen player can then resume walking.

Power Charge

Break into small groups and discuss:

- How can we be like the sheep in the passage we read today?
- What can we do to reach out to others?

Alternate Voltage

Plan an outreach to the community so that children can see firsthand how to show compassion toward others. For example, plan a service day for the senior citizens of your church. Have church members submit projects that they need help with, such as cleaning houses, washing cars, mowing yards, washing windows, etc. Be sure to involve parents for adult supervision and extra help.

Remember Relay

Energy Level Low

Starter

This game focuses on the story of the Last Supper, reminding children that we should remember what Jesus did for us.

Read Luke 22:14–19. Discuss how just before Jesus gave His life for us, He shared a Passover meal with His disciples. The Passover meal was a special celebration for the Jewish people that reminded them of God freeing them from slavery. Jesus wanted to give His disciples a special way to remember what He would do for them. He told them to always remember Him whenever they took wine and bread together. Ask children:

- What did Jesus want His disciples to remember?
- When do we share this special meal together to remember all that Jesus did for us?

Power Tools

- None

Power Source

"And He took bread, gave thanks and broke it, and gave it to them, saying, 'This is my body given for you; do this in remembrance of me.'" Luke 22:19

Bible Story Game

Have the children to sit in two rows a few feet apart. Whisper a phrase or sentence from the lesson to the first child in each row. Each child should whisper the message to the next person in the row until the last person hears the message. Ask the last person in each row to stand and repeat what she heard. Say aloud the original phrase. The group whose phrase best matches the original wins!

Power Charge

Every time we celebrate communion or the Lord's Supper in church, we are telling others what Jesus did for us. Ask children:

- What are some other things that we can do to remind us of all that Jesus said and did for us?

Alternate Voltage

Whisper a different phrase or sentence from Luke 22:19 to each row of children. Additional suggestions are:

- Jesus died on the cross for my sins.
- The Lord's Supper helps me to remember what Jesus did for me.

Scattered

Energy Level Medium

Starter

This game provides an opportunity to teach children about the importance of Jesus' death. Before Jesus' death, we were all separated from God because of our sin. Jesus' death brought us back to God—our sins have been forgiven. His death allows every person to have a relationship with God.

Read Matthew 27:45–54. Discuss how sin separates us from God. Jesus took the punishment for our sins through His death so that we would no longer be separated from God. Share the truth that everyone—no matter how "good" a person he is—needs to be forgiven. Discuss the significance of Jesus' death. Ask children:

- Why did Jesus have to die?
- What did Jesus' death accomplish for us?

Power Tools

- None

Power Source

"For God so loved the world that He gave his one and only Son, that whoever believes in Him shall not perish but have eternal life."
John 3:16

Bible Story Game

Before beginning this game, count how many children are in the group. Have children scatter throughout the room. Make sure they are as far away from each other as possible. Say an odd number if there is an even number of children in the group or an even number if there is an odd number of children. After you say the number, players should run to form groups of that number. Any players not in groups are out of the game. After each round, say "Scatter!", so that the children scatter throughout the room again. Continue to say numbers until there are two or three children left. They are the winners!

Power Charge

Discuss Jesus' death and what it means. Before Jesus' death, we were so far from God that our sin separated us from Him. Just like in the game, we were scattered, far from each other. But God loved us so much, He sent His Son to take the punishment for our sins. We are no longer far from God—we have been brought back to a relationship with Him. Ask children:

- How did Jesus' death pay for our sins?
- What are some ways we can have a close relationship with God?

Alternate Voltage

Announce different actions that the children should perform as they form groups (for example, crab walk, walk backward, walk in slow motion, crawl, etc.).

Egg Run

Energy Level Medium

Starter

This game focuses on Jesus' resurrection and the joy that Mary found in sharing the good news that Jesus was alive.

Read John 20:10–18. Mary was heartbroken because Jesus had died. When she found His empty tomb, she thought someone had moved His body. Then, Jesus appeared to her! He was alive! After talking with Jesus, she ran to tell others. Ask children:

- How do you think Mary felt when she saw that Jesus was alive?

Power Tools

- Plastic spoons
- Plastic eggs
- Masking tape

Power Source

"He said to them, 'Go into all the world and preach the good news to all creation.'" Mark 16:15

Bible Story Game

Divide into two teams. Explain that when the game begins, one player from each team should place a plastic egg in a spoon, carry it quickly to the designated turning point (marked with masking tape), take it back to the start, and give it to the next person on his team while saying, "Jesus is alive!" The game continues until everyone has had a turn. If the egg falls off of the spoon, the player should start again. The first team to complete the relay wins.

Power Charge

Explain that there is no better news than the news of Resurrection Day: Jesus is alive! That's good news to share. We shouldn't walk—we should run—to let others know. Break into small groups and discuss:

- How can you share the good news about Jesus with others?

Alternate Voltage

For an added challenge, have children use real eggs and play the game outside.

Our Final Destination

Energy Level Medium

Starter

In this game, children learn that Heaven is our final destination. As children of God, we have the honor of being accepted into Heaven.

Read Luke 24:50–53. Explain to children that after Jesus died on the cross and rose from the dead, He spent time with His disciples. After 40 days, He ascended to Heaven. He had another destination, and we have another destination too. Even though we live on Earth, one day all believers will join Jesus in Heaven. Ask children:

• What does the word "ascension" mean?

Power Tools

• 2 different sets of paper strips with various clues written on them, such as "Look under the places where people sit" (chairs)

• 2 prizes, such as a bag of candy

Power Source

"So if the Son sets you free, you will be free indeed." John 8:36

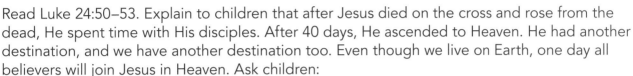

Bible Story Game

Before class, place the clues throughout the room. Place the prizes according to the last clues. Remember that each team should have a set of clues. Divide into two teams. Give each team their first clue. Have teams search for their prizes by following the clues to the final destinations. Allow the teams to enjoy their sweet success.

Power Charge

As believers in Jesus, we have a final destination, or another home. That home is Heaven. In the game today, the children searched for destinations on a map. But if Jesus is their Lord and Savior, their final destination is already determined. They don't have to search for it. They don't have to earn it. Because of God's grace, they already have a place in Heaven.

Alternate Voltage

Copy the Scripture verses in the book of Romans that make up the "Road to Salvation": Romans 3:23, 6:23, 5:8, 10:9, 10:13. Post them around the room. Explain that these special "clues" in the Bible will help children in their journey with Jesus.

Designing Duels

Starter

The game will reinforce the importance of following God's direction, even if we don't fully understand it.

Read Acts 10:9–35. Explain that Peter didn't fully understand the vision, or puzzle, that God gave him, yet he was faithful to do exactly what God told him. Because of his obedience, a Gentile (non-Jewish person) became a believer in Jesus Christ, and Peter finally understood the full picture of God's direction. Ask children:

- Why is it sometimes difficult to follow orders?

- How can you better understand what God wants you to do?

Power Tools

- Sheets of paper with a detailed design, one for each pair

- Blank sheets of paper, one for each pair

- Pencils, one for each pair

Power Source

"And I will put my Spirit in you and move you to follow my decrees and be careful to keep my laws." Ezekiel 36:27

Bible Story Game

Divide into pairs. Have each pair sit back to back. Instruct one partner to look at the design on his paper and describe it to his partner so that his partner can draw it based on his instructions. Give children about five minutes to complete the task. Then, allow them to compare the drawing to the original design.

Power Charge

Remind children that sometimes we must listen carefully to understand what we should be doing. When we don't have all the information, it is hard to do what is expected, and even harder to obey. We may not always understand God's direction in our lives, or fully understand where He is leading us, yet we must listen carefully to Him and be obedient—even when we don't understand the whole picture. Ask children:

- Have you ever felt God directing you to do something without understanding why?

Alternate Voltage

For younger children, complete the activity as a class. Provide each child with a sheet of paper and a pencil and give directions to the class.

Freedom Keys

Energy Level
Medium

Starter

As God's children, we are free. The chains of our sins have been broken. Through the story of the angel freeing Peter from jail, children learn about this great gift of freedom.

Read Acts 12:5–19. Discuss what it means to be free in Christ. Explain that Jesus paid a high price so that we could be free from our sins and have a relationship with God. Ask children:

- Do you know anyone that has been rescued from danger?

Power Tools

- 1 lockable box
- 1 paper bag filled with a variety of keys, paper clips, and small objects that may be used to open a lock
- Correct key to open the lock

Power Source

"So if the Son sets you free, you will be free indeed." John 8:36

Bible Story Game

Have children take turns choosing an object from the bag without looking inside. Give each child a turn to open the box. To keep the suspense, hide the correct key until everyone has tried to unlock the box. Then, slip the key into the bag discreetly and let the children continue taking turns until someone unlocks the box.

Power Charge

Tell children that in the game, they tried many keys and objects to open the box. Explain that just like in their lives, they may sometimes try to be good so that they can get to Heaven. The Bible says that Jesus is the only way—the only key—to Heaven. His death unlocked the way to having a relationship with God, so we can have eternal life with God.

- If there is anyone who still needs salvation, offer to lead him in a prayer that will unlock the door for a relationship with God.

Alternate Voltage

Inside the box, place a special treat and cards for each child with the Power Source verse on them.

8/1/15

Jail Break

Starter

This game recalls the story of Paul and Silas, reminding children about the power of worshipping the Lord in all circumstances.

Read Acts 16:22–26. Discuss how Paul and Silas were beaten and thrown in jail, but they didn't lose their faith. Instead of complaining, they praised the Lord by singing. Then, there was an earthquake, and they were set free! Ask children:

- Do you know praise and worship songs that you can sing to God when trouble comes?

Power Tools

- Music CD
- CD player
- Chairs

Power Source

"But thou art holy, O thou that inhabitest the praises of Israel." Psalm 22:3, kjv

Bible Story Game

Make a "jail" by arranging chairs in a square with an opening at one end for a door. Choose two children to be "jailers." The other children should enter the "jail." Turn on the music and have those in "jail" sing loudly. When you turn off the music and yell, "Earthquake!" the children should run through the "jail" door. The "jailers" should tag as many children as possible in 10 seconds. Each tagged child should return to "jail." Turn on the music to signal the end of the round. All children not tagged become the new "jailers".

Power Charge

Discuss how Paul and Silas may have been in chains, yet they still sang songs to God. Even in times of trouble, we should sing praises to God for all that He has done for us. Sing some praise and worship songs together, lifting up the Lord. Ask the children to share their favorite praise and worship songs.

Alternate Voltage

Play a portion of a familiar praise and worship song. At any point, abruptly stop the song and give children an opportunity to sing the next line.

Blind Faith

Energy Level Low

Starter

This game teaches children about Paul's conversion, one of the Bible's greatest examples of God's life-changing power—and how that power can change their lives.

Read Acts 22:6–16. Explain that before this point, Paul was called Saul, and he persecuted Christians. He had even given his approval when Stephen was martyred. But, Paul had an encounter with Jesus that changed his life. After Paul's encounter with Jesus, he became a devoted follower of Christ. He wrote most of the New Testament. God's truth changes lives. Ask children:

- How do you think Paul's life changed after this experience?

- How has being a Christian changed your life?

Power Tools

- Two shoe boxes
- Two blindfolds
- Two pencils
- Two rulers
- Two rolls of tape
- Two baseballs
- Two pieces of bubble gum

Power Source

"Guide me in your truth and teach me, for you are God my Savior, and my hope is in you all day long." Psalm 25:5

Bible Story Game

Divide into two teams. Blindfold one player from each team. Give teach team a box containing one of each item listed above. Explain that each team should carefully give teach item to their blindfolded teammate. The blindfolded teammate should attempt to identify each item. The first team to correctly identify all five items wins.

Power Charge

Remind children that before salvation, all of us were blind. Though Paul experienced physical blindness for three days during his conversion, all of us were spiritually blind before Jesus brought light to our lives. We were in darkness. When Jesus saved us, He gave us light and hope. Break into small groups and discuss:

- How has Jesus changed your life?

- What kind of things can we "see" when we have Jesus in our lives?

Alternate Voltage

Invite an adult to share her life-changing testimony with children as a way to encourage their faith.

Shipwrecked!

Energy Level Medium

Starter

This game uses the story of Paul's shipwreck to demonstrate that even when things go bad, God is watching over you. When Paul was a prisoner on a boat, there was a hurricane. Everyone on board thought that they would die, but Paul assured them that God told him they would live. God made sure that every person on that boat made it to safety.

Read Acts 27:13–26, 41–44. Ask children:

- How did God protect Paul?

Power Tools

- 2 25-ft. (8 m) lengths of yarn
- 2 toy rings

Power Source

"The Lord will keep you from all harm—he will watch over your life; the Lord will watch over your coming and going both now and forevermore." Psalm 121:7–8

Bible Story Game

Divide into two teams. Give each team a length of yarn. Have each team stand in a straight line, side by side. Have each team weave the yarn from one person to the next. It should go through belt loops, shoelace loops, around backs, legs, arms, etc. Give the first member of each team a ring. When you say, "Go!" the children should weave the yarn through the ring to bring "Paul's boat" to "shore" without getting "shipwrecked." The first team to safely get the ring to the end wins.

Power Charge

Explain that even when things go wrong, God is still watching over us. Paul was a prisoner in a hurricane and had a shipwreck, but God still made sure he was safe. God will do the same for us. Break into small groups and discuss:

- When was a time you know God was watching over you?
- How can you be aware of God's hand in your life?

Alternate Voltage

When the players start weaving the yarn, instruct them to either create more or less loops, depending on how challenging you want the game to be.

Quick Change

Energy Level

High

Starter

This game reminds children that there are two ways to clothe themselves: physically and spiritually. God wants us to be sure that we wear our spiritual clothes every day too.

Read Colossians 3:12–14. Discuss how everyone wears clothes, but the Bible tells us to wear another set of clothes—clothes that we can't see. The Bible tells us to clothe ourselves with compassion, kindness, humility, gentleness, and patience. These "spiritual clothes" help others see God's love and presence in our lives while helping to point others to Jesus. Ask children:

- How can we clothe ourselves in kindness? Humility? Patience?
- Why do you think Paul said to put on these qualities like we put on clothing?
- According to Scripture, what binds all of the spiritual clothing together? (love)

Power Tools

- 2 clothes baskets
- 2 mismatched men's outfits (including hats, pants, shoes, and jackets)

Power Source

"For all of you who were baptized into Christ have clothed yourselves with Christ." Galatians 3:27

Bible Story Game

Take turns having two children play this game at one time. Have the other children cheer them on. Explain that the two players should remove their shoes. Then, when you say, "Go!" they race against each other to put all of the clothes in their clothes basket on over their regular clothes. The first player to wear all of the clothes wins.

Power Charge

Explain that just like we put on clothing every day like shirts, shoes, belts, etc., we should also put on our spiritual clothing like gentleness, patience, and compassion, etc. The spiritual clothing we wear is an example of Jesus' love to those around us.

Read Colossians 3:12-14. Invite each child to select a piece of clothing from the clothes baskets. Ask them to describe what "spiritual garment" they have chosen and how it would look to others. For example, a shirt could be a garment of kindness that others would see when he helped a friend carry heavy books; a coat could be a garment of patience that others would see as she played outdoor games with her younger sibling.

Alternate Voltage

Add extra clothing to make it harder, such as gloves, neckties, rubber galoshes, etc.

Fruit Baskets

Starter

This game helps children identify the fruit of the Spirit by name and in their lives.

Read Galatians 5:22–23. The fruit of the Spirit are forces that God puts inside of us when we choose to be a follower of Christ. They are spiritual forces that help us to live powerful lives and cause others to see Jesus in us. Ask children:

• Which fruit of the spirit are most evident in your life?

Power Tools

• 2 fruit baskets

• 18 pieces of fruit (real or plastic)

• A small sticker on each fruit that lists one of the fruit of the Spirit from Galatians 5:22–23

Power Source

The fruit of the Spirit is love, joy, peace, patience, kindness, goodness, faithfulness, gentleness and self-control.
Galatians 5:22–23

Bible Story Game

Take turns having two players play while the others watch. Explain that two children should race against each other to remove the labeled fruit from their baskets one at a time, run across the room, and place them in order, according to the verse. The first player to get all of her fruit in order wins.

Power Charge

Explain that the fruit of the Spirit is something that we can develop in our lives through practice and prayer. As we do, the fruit grows stronger and sweeter, and so do we! Break into small groups and discuss one or more of the fruit of the Spirit. Then, regroup and have each group share a definition of each fruit, as well as ways that it can be nurtured and matured through practice.

Alternate Voltage

To make the game more or less challenging, hide the Scripture while playing or make the Scripture available for children to view.

Fruit Scramble

Energy Level Medium

Starter

This game reinforces the importance of working together.

Read Ephesians 4:11–16. Remind children that everyone has a part to play in the body of Christ. Every role is equally important. If we work together, we can impact the world for Christ. Ask children:

- Why do you think people have different roles in the body of Christ?
- How do they work together?

Power Tools

- Fruit-flavored ring cereal
- 2 large bowls

Power Source

"Instead, speaking the truth in love, we will in all things grow up into him who is the Head, that is, Christ. From him the whole body, joined and held together by every supporting ligament, grows and builds itself up in love, as each part does its work."
Ephesians 4:15–16

Bible Story Game

Divide players into teams of five or more. Explain that one person on each team is the gatherer, and the others are the counters. At the start of the game, the gatherer should take pieces of cereal from the bowl and separate them by color. Each counter should count and collect 25 pieces of each color. Remind children that they should cooperate. The first team to collect 25 pieces of four different colors wins.

Power Charge

Review the Power Source verse. Ask children:

- How well did your teams work together to win this game?
- Why do you think it is important to work together and encourage each other as we do the work Christ called us to do? What if we tried to do this work on our own?
- What role do children play as members of Christ's church body?

Alternate Voltage

Invite guest speakers to discuss their roles in the body of Christ (for example, a pastor, missionary, church administrator, teacher, evangelist, etc.). Explain to children what each title means and what gifts each one requires.

Follow the Leader

Starter

This game looks at Paul's admonition to follow Christ's example, as well as the example of those who are following Christ.

Read Ephesians 5:1–21. Discuss how we should be imitators of God, living like Jesus did. We should want to live differently than the world, pure and holy, and seeking God in all we do. Ask children:

- What are some examples of how Jesus lived?
- How can we live like He did?

Power Tools

- None

Power Source

"Follow my example, as I follow the example of Christ."
1 Corinthians 11:1

Bible Story Game

Explain that for this game, children should imitate you. Lead children in a series of 10 steps, such as hopping, skipping, jumping, turning around, etc. After completing the first round, add on a new step. Continue until most children have difficulty repeating the steps. See how well children can follow your example.

Power Charge

Explain that God not only wants us to follow Him, He wants us to live lives worthy of imitation. By living a good life, others will learn what it is like to live for God and see God in you. Ask children:

- Can you think of someone who looks up to you?
- What kind of example are you to them?

Alternate Voltage

Vary the game by playing Guess the Leader. Have children stand in a circle. Select one child to be the guesser who should leave the room briefly while a leader is chosen. The guesser stands in the center of the circle. Everyone starts marching in place. The leader should eventually perform another movement. Everyone will quickly imitate the leader as she performs additional movements. The guesser must try to identify the leader based on what he observes.

Armor Action Game

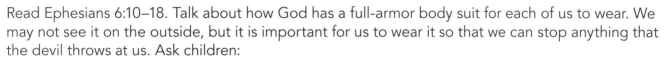

Energy Level

High

Starter

This game emphasizes the armor of God; it teaches children the various parts and significance of God's armor.

Read Ephesians 6:10–18. Talk about how God has a full-armor body suit for each of us to wear. We may not see it on the outside, but it is important for us to wear it so that we can stop anything that the devil throws at us. Ask children:

- How can you "put on" the armor of God?

Power Tools

- 2 badminton racquets
- 10 crumpled sheets of red paper
- 10 crumpled sheets of orange paper

Power Source

"Put on the full armor of God so that you can take your stand against the devil's schemes." Ephesians 6:11

Bible Story Game

Divide into pairs. Allow two pairs to play at one time. Have teams stand several feet (2-3 meters) apart facing each other. Explain that one player should throw paper balls, pretending that they are fiery darts, to his teammate while she swings with the racquet. The team that hits the most paper balls wins.

Power Charge

Explain that God has us wearing His truth, righteousness, faith, readiness, salvation, and Word like an armor of protection. He knows that when these things are active in our lives, we won't fall. We'll stand strong! Break into small groups and discuss:

- After Paul described the armor of God, he said we should pray. Why is that?
- What does it mean to wear a helmet of salvation? A breastplate of righteousness? A belt of truth? A shield of faith? Feet fitted with readiness?
- Why is God's Word called a sword?

Alternate Voltage

Instead of teams, take turns having several children toss the paper balls in rapid succession as the players try to hit all them.

Only Good Things

Energy Level Low

Starter

Many things in our culture compete for our attention and take our focus from living for God. This game reminds children of Paul's words, encouraging us to protect our minds by thinking about things that honor God.

Read Philippians 4:8. Explain that in order to think about things that honor God, we should be careful about what we take into our minds. Instead of dwelling on things that may displease God—movies, video games, TV shows, gossip, etc.—we should concentrate on things that glorify Him. Ask children:

- How do our thoughts affect how we live?

Power Tools

- Poster displaying a variety of items
- Paper, one sheet per child
- Pens or pencils, one per child
- Stopwatch

Power Source

"Finally, brothers, whatever is true, whatever is noble, whatever is right, whatever is pure, whatever is lovely, whatever is admirable—if anything is excellent or praiseworthy—think about such things." Philippians 4:8

Bible Story Game

Distribute paper and pens to children. Allow the players 10 seconds to study the poster. Then, remove it. Give the players one minute to list everything that they remember. The child who correctly records the most items from the picture wins.

Power Charge

Break into small groups. Ask children:

- Why is it important for us to guard the things we see and hear?
- How can we ensure that we'll think about things that are true, noble, right, pure, lovely, and admirable?

Alternate Voltage

Use this opportunity to talk about peer pressure, both positive and negative. Discuss how guarding our minds can help us to avoid pressure from compromising situations.

Rope Race

Energy Level
Medium

Starter

This game encourages children to be gentle so that others can experience God's love through them. The way we deal with people every day is one of the greatest witnesses that we have. More than what we say, our gentleness—our unselfishness and patience—will speak volumes about the change that God has made in our lives.

Read Philippians 4:4–7. Explain to the children that the apostle Paul was telling the church at Philippi how to behave, and these verses address how to treat others. If we treat others with respect, patience, and gentleness, they will see the difference that God has made in our lives. Ask children:

- What do our actions say about us?

- Can people see that you love Jesus by the way you act?

Power Tools

- Modeling clay
- 2 smooth surfaces
- Masking tape
- Measuring tape
- Stopwatch

Power Source

"Let your gentleness be evident to all." Philippians 4:5

Bible Story Game

Divide into pairs. Allow two pairs to play at a time. Using masking tape, mark a finish line several feet from the starting area. Give each team an equal amount of modeling clay. Each team should have two minutes to shape the clay into the longest possible rope. Then, while each player holds one end of the clay rope, they should carry it over the finish line without breaking it. If the rope breaks before the pair crosses the finish line, they should start over. The team with the longest rope that crosses the finish line first wins.

Power Charge

Discuss ways that children can exhibit gentleness to others. Explore different scenarios—at home, at school, with friends, during extracurricular activities.

Alternate Voltage

Use mounds of pizza dough instead of modeling clay. Have teams race to make the biggest circle of pizza dough. Consider ending with a pizza party.

Get Ready!

Starter

This game, from the gospel of Matthew, reminds children that Jesus is returning, and that we should be prepared for Him.

Read Matthew 24:30, 42-44. Let children know that when Jesus went into Heaven, it was not the end. The Bible tells us that He will come again to retrieve the church. Although we do not know when Jesus will return, we need to be watchful and prepared for this day. Ask children:

• Why should we be prepared for Jesus' return?

Power Tools

• Sheets of paper, one per child

• Pens or pencils, one per child

• Stopwatch

Power Source

"So you also must be ready, because the Son of Man will come at an hour when you do not expect him." Matthew 24:44

Bible Story Game

Divide into teams of two or three. Distribute paper and a pen to each child. Pick an event such as going to a party, the first day of school, having a garage sale, going on a long vacation. Explain that when you say "Go!" each child has one minute to write the most important ways to be prepared for the event. Ways to be prepared may include things to do before leaving, things to bring, etc. After one minute, have players on each team compare lists to see if they matched responses. Each match between players scores one point. The team with the most points wins the round. Choose another event and play again.

Power Charge

Explain that the game required the children to list how they would get ready for special events. Break into small groups and discuss:

• Have you ever felt unprepared for something?

• What happened as a result of being unprepared?

• What does it mean to be ready for Jesus' return?

Alternate Voltage

As a final event in the game, use "preparing for the return of Jesus." Discuss ways to get ready for this very special event such as: encourage each another; read the Bible every day; obey God's commands, etc.

Crazy Relay

Ene
Lev
High

Starter

This game reminds children of the instructions Paul gave Timothy—to be a good example and not to forsake his gift.

Read 1 Timothy 4:12, 14–16. Talk about how Paul instructed Timothy to be an example to others even though he was young. God wants each of us, no matter our age, to be an example of Him. Ask children:

- Why is it important for you to be a good example to those around you?

- What are some gifts you have?

Power Tools

- 2 paper bags or boxes

- Slips of paper with crazy action instructions written on each (Prepare as many instructions as there are players. See *Alternate Voltage* for examples.)

Power Source

"Don't let anyone look down on you because you are young, but set an example for the believers in speech, in life, in love, in faith and in purity." 1 Timothy 4:12

Bible Story Game

Divide into two teams. Have each team form a single file line. Place the bag or box filled with the crazy actions about 10–12 feet in front of each team. Explain that when you say "Go!" the first player from each team should run to the bag, choose a slip of paper, and do what it says as quickly as possible. His team should follow his example and repeat the action. The player continues the action until all of his teammates join him. Upon completion, the player races back to his team and tags the next player. Play continues until one team completes all of the instructions in the bag.

Power Charge

Explain that God wants us to be good examples so that others will see Jesus in us. Break into small groups and discuss:

- Describe a situation when you provided a good example to someone?

Alternate Voltage

For older children, allow them to prepare the slips.

Crazy Action examples:

- Hop up and down five times yelling, "This is crazy!"

- Race to a player on another team and shake her hand three times.

Entangled

Starter

This game focuses on the teaching in Hebrews that sin hinders and entangles us.

Read Hebrews 12:1–11. Talk about how sin entangles us and keeps us from running the race that God planned for us. God wants us to throw off all sin and fix our eyes on Jesus, who will help us grow strong in Him. Ask children:

- What does it mean when we say sin "entangles"?
- What does the Bible mean when it says we should "fix our eyes on Jesus"?

Power Tools

- None

Power Source

"Since we are surrounded by such a great cloud of witnesses, let us throw off everything that hinders and the sin that so easily entangles, and let us run with perseverance the race marked out for us." Hebrews 12:1

Bible Story Game

Divide into two teams. Explain that each team should stand in a circle. Each player should put his right hand in the circle and hold the hand of someone else in the circle, but not anyone beside him. Then, each player should put his left hand in the circle, this time grabbing the hand of a different player, but not anyone beside him. When you say, "Go!" each team should "untangle" without letting go of any hands. This will require them to go under and over each other's arms. The first team to untangle wins.

Power Charge

Explain that if we have sinned and our lives seem tangled, we shouldn't lose hope. God forgives us when we ask, and He will help us be free of anything that keeps us from Him. According to the Scripture, He knows our struggles and encourages us to be strong and not to give up. Break into small groups and discuss:

- What are some things that can hinder, or prevent us, from being all God wants us to be?
- How can fixing our eyes on Jesus help keep us from becoming entangled in sin?

Alternate Voltage

For younger children, divide teams into smaller groups before including everyone in the game.

The Teaching of James

Jumping through Hoops

Energy Level Medium

Starter

This game is based on James' teaching that emphasizes that we can know God and that He hears us. We don't have to go to impossible lengths to know Him—we just have to open our lives to Him.

Read Matthew 7:7–8, James 4:8, and 1 John 5:13–15. Talk about how God doesn't make it difficult for us to get to know Him. He wants to know each of us personally—and He said all we have to do is come near to God by talking with Him. We don't have to jump through hoops. Ask children:

- What are some things you can talk to God about?

Power Tools

- Large toy hoop

Power Source

"Come near to God and he will come near to you." James 4:8

Bible Story Game

Have the children form a circle and hold hands. Give the hoop to a volunteer and ask her to loop it over her arm before holding hands with the person next to them. Explain that the players should then move the hoop around the circle without letting go of each other's hands. They should step through the hoop and move it over their arms, shoulders, head, etc.

Power Charge

Explain that there are many ways to get to know God. We shouldn't forget that, more than anything, God just wants us to talk to Him and let Him talk to us. God desires to have a personal relationship with us. When we seek Him and turn to Him, He will speak to our hearts and share His truth with us. Break into small groups and discuss:

- What does it mean to pray "according to His will"?
- What are some ways God can speak to us?

Alternate Voltage

Divide into two teams and use two hoops. The first team to get the hoop around their circle back to the starting player without letting go of each other's hands wins. Or, play this game as a class using two different-sized hoops that travel in different directions.

The Roar of the Lion

Energy Level Medium

Starter

From this teaching in 1 Peter, children discover that Satan is real, and his goal is to cause destruction. The Bible tells us to be alert and strong in our faith and trust in God's mighty power. Read 1 Peter 5:6–11. Explain to the children that we have an enemy in the world—Satan. The Bible compares him to a roaring lion; he wants to pull us away from God. If we stand firm in our faith and turn to God for the strength to resist, we don't have to be afraid. God's power and love are stronger than anything the enemy can do. Ask children:

- Why does this Scripture tells us to be alert?
- How could the enemy "devour" us?

Power Tools

- Prizes, such as ribbons or buttons

Power Source

"Be self-controlled and alert. Your enemy the devil prowls around like a roaring lion looking for someone to devour." 1 Peter 5:8

Bible Story Game

Choose three leaders to be judges. Then, invite children to show off their best lion roars. Award prizes to all children who participate. Give special prizes for:

Most Realistic Roar	Gentlest Roar
Loudest Roar	Most Animated Roar
Silliest Roar	Scariest Roar

Power Charge

Emphasize that this was a silly roaring game. In reality, Satan can make a lot of noise in our lives and is serious in trying to keep us from God. Ask children:

- What kind of "noise" does Satan make in our lives?
- In 1 Peter 5:9, it says for us to "Resist him, standing firm in the faith . . . " What are some things we can do to resist Satan?

Alternate Voltage

Play a game of "Lion Tag." Place a Bible on a table and designate it to be the "Standing Firm" Safe Zone. Have a volunteer be the "lion." The "lion" will attempt to keep all players from reaching the Safe Zone. If a player is tagged, he should freeze until another player tags him to set him free. A player cannot be tagged within the Safe Zone. The game ends when all the players have reached the Safe Zone.

Moving Heaven and Earth

Energy Level Medium

Starter

This game introduces children to the book of Revelation, showing them that no matter how hard things may seem, God has a hopeful future for them.

Read Revelation 21:1–5. Explain that God gave a vision of the future to the apostle John. Specifically, God showed John that one day, there would be a new Heaven and a new Earth and that all of the bad things would go away. There wouldn't be anymore pain, or death, or crying. Ask children:

- What is something that you are looking forward to when God makes a new Heaven and a new Earth?

Power Tools

- None

Power Source

"'He will wipe every tear from their eyes. There will be no more death or mourning or crying or pain, for the old order of things has passed away.'" Revelation 21:4

Bible Story Game

Instruct children to stand in rows. Explain that they should crouch when you say "New Earth" and stand when you say "New Heaven." If they stand when they should sit or vice versa, they are out. As the game progresses, go faster, mixing up the order in which you say the words. The last one standing (or sitting) wins.

Power Charge

Explain that there are many terrible things in this world because sin has made a mess. God has hope for His children, not only in the here and now, but in the future. He has a perfect future for each of us—in a new Heaven and a new Earth. Break into small groups and discuss:

- What does God mean when He says that He will wipe every tear from our eyes?
- Will everyone see the new Heaven and the new Earth?

Alternate Voltage

Add a challenge to the game by playing energetic praise and worship music during the game. Have the children move around the room as the music plays. Keep the children alert and listening by saying "New Earth" or "New Heaven" randomly as the music plays. Anyone who does not complete the correct action or is the last to complete the action is out.

We "Knee-d" Rain

Energy Level Medium

Starter

In this game children can discuss God's faithfulness to provide for our needs.

Read Jeremiah 5:24. Talk about the four seasons, what kind of weather they bring, and how trees and plants change through the seasons. Ask children:

- How important is rain to plants and animals?
- God is faithful to bring us the seasons right on time How has God been faithful to provide for your other needs?

Power Tools

- None

Power Source

"'Let us fear the Lord our God, who gives autumn and spring rains in season.'" Jeremiah 5:24

Icebreaker Game

Have children sit in two or three groups. Stand in front of the children, facing them. Show how to produce different rainfall sounds. Have the first group begin snapping their fingers, producing the sounds of the first raindrops. As the first group continues snapping, shave the middle group start snapping, then the third. Next, one at a time, have groups begin knee pats as the rainfall grows heavier. Then, "conduct" the raindrop orchestra, all of them at once, raising your arms for harder knee pats to make the storm increase, then lowering your arms to soften the knee pats, and soften the storm effect. To end the activity, reverse the order, heavy knee pats, soft knee pats, snapping, and then, group by group, silence. Save the last snap for you—the last drop to fall.

Power Charge

Ask children:

- How does rain provide for our needs today?
- What does it mean that God provides our needs "in season"?
- Explain that we don't always get what we want, or need, exactly at the time we think is best. Sometimes we have to wait and trust Him for His perfect timing.

Alternate Voltage

Add some extra details to the storm by having children swish their palms together, make a "shhhhh" sound, or, for thunder, tap on plastic containers.

Find Five

Starter

God handmade each of His children. We are wonderfully made. Each one of us is a masterpiece—the work of the Master Artist.

Read Psalm 139:14 which calls our lives the work of the Master Artist. Ask children:

- Do you think that each person is like a beautiful piece of artwork that God has made? In what ways?

- What does it mean to you when the Bible says that we are "wonderfully made"?

- What kinds of things can we say to help others realize that they are wonderfully made?

Power Tools

- Music CD
- CD player
- 2 potatoes

Power Source

"I praise You because I am fearfully and wonderfully made; Your works are wonderful, I know that full well." Psalm 139:14

Icebreaker Game

Assign each child a number so that there are two children per number. Tell them they have one minute of music to find the child with the same number. Once each child has found his partner, have each pair share and memorize five things about each other. After three minutes, direct everyone to form a large circle. Turn on the music and pass two potatoes around the circle. Stop the music. Each child holding a potato should introduce her partner and tell five things about him. Play until everyone has been introduced.

For younger children, have them memorize two things about their partners.

Power Charge

Ask children:

- Why do you think God made each of us unique?

- Comment that every potato is different. All of them are useful for making a variety of unique potato dishes, such as chips, fries, or mashed potatoes, etc. Does God have a special plan for each of us? What do you hope His plan is for you?

Alternate Voltage

List 10 things for children to discover about each other. Include some serious and some off-the-wall things (name of first pet, favorite cartoon, color of house, etc.). Have the children choose which five they will use.

Icing on the Cake

Energy Level
Medium

Starter

In this world driven by competition, glamour, and possessions, it is vital to instill in children that what really matters in life is knowing that our value comes from God. This game makes learning that truth delicious.

Read Job 10:8. Ask children:

- What things have you made with your hands? (Encourage children to tell how proud they felt about their creations.)
- God puts within us the talents, interests, ideas, and emotions that He wants in our life. If you were to write Him a thank-you card for making you, what would you say?

Power Tools

- A large poster board with a drawn outline of a large cupcake (Leave open areas within the cake area and within the icing area for words to be written.)
- Cupcakes, without icing
- Icing and sprinkles
- Plastic knives for spreading icing

Power Source

"Your hands shaped me and made me." Job 10:8

Icebreaker Game

Display the drawing of the cupcake. Ask children what makes up their daily lives (their likes and dislikes, the everyday things they do, if they had homework, etc.). Some of these should be everyday things that most children do. Write these shared things on the "cake" part of the drawing. Then, have children share their unique talents, hobbies, and dreams for the future. Write those items in the icing part of the drawing. These are the icing on the cake! Tell the children that we should celebrate God's goodness and creativity for giving each of us one-of-a-kind qualities that top our life with sweetness! Close the activity by spreading icing on each cupcake. Enjoy the cupcakes as a snack.

Power Charge

Ask children:

- What kind of world would it be if we were all the same?
- How did God make the first man, forming and shaping Him? (See Genesis 2:7.)
- On days when things go wrong, how can you remind yourself that God made you the "icing on the cake"?
- How can you encourage others about God's great love and plan for them?

Name Game Rap

Energy Level Medium

Starter

Here's a fun rap game to remind children that their walk with God is the biggest and best part of their lives. It will also help them to remember how special they are as new creations in Him.

Read 2 Corinthians 5:17, and compare it to the life cycle of the caterpillar. Once a caterpillar is a butterfly, he doesn't act or think like a caterpillar anymore. Sometimes, however, Christians can forget we are new creations. Thankfully, we have God's Word, filled with promises and truth, that remind us every day that we are new creations in Christ. Ask children:

- What does it mean to be a new creation in Christ?
- We sometimes forget how important God is in our lives. How can we remind ourselves that life is really all about Him?

Power Tools

- Copies of Rap Worksheet (see page 110), one per child
- Pens or pencils, one per child

Power Source

"Therefore, if anyone is in Christ, he is a new creation; the old has gone, the new has come!" 2 Corinthians 5:17

Icebreaker Game

Divide into pairs. Allow children to spend a few minutes learning about each other. Give the Rap Worksheet to each child to complete about her partner. Then, have each child perform a rap about her partner while a few children become the band and beat rhythms. Tell the band to use knee slaps, mouth noises, hand claps, etc. Encourage children to relax and have fun with this activity. Have the audience clap along.

Power Charge

Review the Power Source verse. Ask children:

- What do you think the verse means by saying, "the old has gone, and the new has come"?
- Are there some "old" things in your life that need to be replaced by new things?
- What are some of the ways that God works His newness in our lives?

Alternate Voltage

Record the children's raps, then listen to it again as a group.

Rap Worksheet

This is _____ and this is his/her rap.
He/She's a Christian and a real cool cat.

He/She likes to _____ and he/she likes to _____ .
He/She likes _____ for breakfast and _____
to munch. He/She likes _____ for dinner and
_____ for lunch.

He/She loves the Lord, oh yeah. As a Christian, here's what he/
she likes to do: _____ on Sunday, _____ on
other days too, _____ in the meantime, and _____
if he/she's feelin' blue.

What does God mean to him/her? Well, God is really fine. God is
_____ and _____ and _____ and _____ and
_____, and now we're out of time.

This is _____, I introduce to you,
a really cool Christian and an awesome friend too.

Sheep to Sheep

Energy Level Medium

Starter

This game makes it fun for "sheep" to get acquainted with each other. As the Good Shepherd, Jesus knows His sheep well. Every hair is numbered, every thought and action known.

Read John 10:3–5, 14. Talk about the role of a shepherd and what he does for his sheep. Touch on the importance of knowing Christ and each other. Ask children:

- Have you ever seen a real sheep? Did all of the sheep look alike to you?
- Jesus says He knows His sheep. What are some of the ways that we can get to know Him better?
- What are some ways that we can get to know each other better?

Power Tools

- Colorful index cards with "Sheep named ____" written on the fronts, one per child
- Pencils, one per child

Power Source

"I am the good shepherd; I know my sheep and my sheep know me." John 10:14

Icebreaker Game

Have each child write his name on the front of the card and three brief things about himself on the back. Review each card for readability and content. Shuffle the cards and distribute them to children. Instruct children to look only at the name on the front of the card. Explain that when you say "Go!" children should find the sheep whose card he is holding, by calling out "BAAA!" and each fact on the back of the card. They should not say the name. See how long it takes for the sheep to find each other in the noise of the flock.

Power Charge

Review the Power Source verse. Ask children:

- Why do you think it's important for us to get to know our church friends?
- Have you ever felt like a "lost sheep" at a new church? What helped you to make new friends?
- How well do you know Jesus? What can you do to get to know Him better?

Alternate Voltage

Create categories for the children to write about, for example, favorite bands or music, three places they would like to visit, favorite foods, etc.

Open Chair Dare

Starter

This game provides a lesson in putting others first.

Read Philippians 2:3. Ask children:

- What does the word "humility" mean to you?
- How do we show people that we value them above ourselves?
- Can you think of times when Jesus valued other people more than Himself?

Power Tools

- Chairs arranged in a circle, facing out, with one less chair than the number of players
- Music CD
- CD player
- Box of snacks (arranged so that players won't know what they are receiving)

Power Source

"In humility consider others better than yourselves." Philippians 2:3

Icebreaker Game

Gather children around the chairs. Explain that when the music starts, players should walk around the circle until the music stops. At that point, two children should try to get to the empty chair. Whether they arrive at the same time, or one arrives first, one should choose to be humble and bow out of the game. Remove a chair for the next round. As the humble person walks away from the chair, secretly give her a special snack. Continue until there is only one player left sitting. Then, have the "humble" players share how they were rewarded for their kind play.

Power Charge

Ask children:

- Is it easy or difficult to show humility?
- Can you tell about a time in your life when it wasn't easy but you put someone else's needs above your own?
- Can you think of a time when someone did that for you? How did it make you feel?

Alternate Voltage

During the game, play different styles of music. Have children move walk to the beat and style of the music—marching for marching music, jumping for exciting praise and worship music, dancing for hip-hop music, etc.

Two Cool, Two Cookies

Energy Level

Low

Starter

In this simple get-to-know-you game, children discover a few threads of God's grand design in the lives of others.

Read Psalm 139:13. Have a tapestry or weaving on display to illustrate the idea of a complex pattern woven into one piece of work. Explain how, like the weaving, we were knitted together by God's own hand. Ask children:

- Have you ever watched someone knit or weave something together?
- When the Bible says that God knitted us together, what does that mean?

Power Tools

- Copies of the Two Cool, Two Cookies worksheet (see page 114), one per child
- Pen or pencil, one per child
- Cookies, 2 per child

Power Source

"For you created my inmost being; you knit me together in my mother's womb." Psalm 139:13

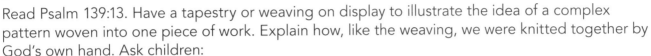

Icebreaker Game

Give each child a copy of the Two Cool, Two Cookies worksheet and a pencil. Instruct children to interview two other children and complete the worksheet with their answers. Explain that, for each child, they should discover and write two cool things, two Christ-like things, two things that child has created, two ways that child wants to change, and two of that child's favorite cartoon characters. Tell children that once this is completed, they should sign the ticket on the worksheet and redeem it for two delicious cookies at the end of class.

Power Charge

Review the Power Source verse. Ask children:

- How does it make you feel to know that God "knit" you together with a unique and wonderful mix of talents, interests, and abilities?
- Think about the two changes you shared during the activity. How do you plan to make these important changes in your life?

Alternate Voltage

Distribute extra copies of the Two Cool, Two Cookies worksheets for children to use to interview two family members.

Two Cool, Two Cookies

	_____ (name)	_____ (name)
Two Cool	_____ _____	_____ _____
Two Christ-Like	_____ _____	_____ _____
Two Creations	_____ _____	_____ _____
Two Changes	_____ _____	_____ _____
Two Cartoons	_____ _____	_____ _____

Two Cookies Coupon

Good for Two Cookies

_____
(approved by)

Two Cookies Coupon

CD-204072 • *180 Faith-Charged Games* • © Carson-Dellosa

Food Gratitude

Energy Level
Medium

Starter

This activity helps children get to know each other while instilling gratitude for the daily bread we receive from the Lord.

Read Exodus 16:15 and Luke 11:3. Explain that the bread or manna that the Lord gave the Israelites every morning in the wilderness was not spectacular, but it was God's daily provision. Without it, they would have surely perished in the desert. In biblical times, bread was an essential part, and sometimes the only part, of the meal. Ask children:

- What kinds of meals do you eat?
- What is your favorite snack? Favorite healthy food? Your least favorite food?
- Do you sometimes take the meals you have for granted? How grateful are you for the daily provision of food? How do you show your gratefulness?

Power Tools

- Music CD with fun, energetic music
- CD player

Power Source

"Moses said to them, 'It is the bread the Lord has given you to eat.'" Exodus 16:15

"Give us each day our daily bread." Luke 11:3

Icebreaker Game

Ask the question, "What is your favorite food?" After the responses, turn on the music and have children wander around the room, shouting the names of their favorite foods until they assemble into groups by food choice. Once in their groups, stop the music. Then, give them several minutes to learn each other's names. As a group, have them say a prayer of gratitude for the "daily bread" that God provides.

Power Charge

Review the Power Source verses. Have children break up into two groups and create two different humorous skits. One will show the Israelites finding manna on the ground every morning and making fun of it, but later wishing they had been grateful. The other skit will show the same scene, except they will have grateful hearts, and that attitude makes the manna taste better. Ask children:

- How can we get an attitude of gratitude for our daily food?
- What kind of prayer do you pray before you eat?

Alternate Voltage

Repeat the game using a favorite activity, favorite color, favorite sport, etc.

The Sound in Your Hand

Energy Level
Medium

Starter

This icebreaker works wonders for gathering children' energy and attention. It also showcases God's amazing creation as heard in the sounds of the variety of animals He made.

Read Song of Songs 2:12 and talk about the amazing sounds of the animals God created. Ask children:

- What is your favorite animal sound?
- Why do you think God created animals with the ability to make unique sounds?

Power Tools

- None

Power Source

"Flowers appear on the earth; the season of singing has come, the cooing of doves is heard in our land." Song of Songs 2:12

Icebreaker Game

Ask children to practice making animal noises. After a few minutes, ask them to stop. Choose two animal sounds. Explain that you will "hold" one animal sound in each hand. Explain that the children should only make an animal sound when you open a hand to let the sound "escape." At any other time, they should be silent. Explain that they can make noise as long your hand stays open. Remind them that they should make two different sounds, depending on which hand you open. Repeat the game by choosing additional pairs of animal sounds.

Power Charge

Review the Power Source verse. Ask children:

- How do you think God feels when you lift your unique voice in praise and worship?

Alternate Voltage

Select specific types of animals each time (for example, farm animals, jungle animals, birds, etc.). Allow volunteers to lead the group.

"You-la" Hoops

Starter

God invented laughter, and the Bible teaches that a cheerful heart is beneficial for our physical well-being. Here's a cheery game using laughter to help children become acquainted.

Read Proverbs 17:22. Explain that laughter is like a breath mint: it freshens our lives, turns frowns upside down, and spreads refreshment to those around us. Ask children:

- What do you think it means when the Bible says that a cheerful heart helps us like medicine?
- Was there a time when God used laughter to cheer you up?

Power Tools

- 4 large toy hoops
- Music CD
- CD player

Power Source

"A cheerful heart is good medicine."
Proverbs 17:22

Icebreaker Game

Have children think of funny stories. Explain that they will have a chance to share them. Turn on the music and have four children twirl hoops at the front of the room. (Those who can't keep the hoops on their waists can twirl them on their arms.) Have the children freeze when the music stops. While frozen, allow each child to tell his name and his story. Switch to a new group of four children and play the game until everyone has told her name and her story.

Power Charge

Review the Power Source verse. Ask children:

- How do you feel after you have laughed?
- Everyone has a different sense of humor. What makes you laugh? How do you make others laugh?

Alternate Voltages

For a real challenge, see how many hoops each child can keep twirling for at least one minute.

8-16-15

Cotton Ball Scoop

Energy Level Medium

Starter

It's not easy to scoop a cotton ball, keep it in a scoop, and place it into a bowl on your head—especially when you're blindfolded! That is, unless somebody helps you, like the Holy Spirit helps all of us.

Read John 14:16. Explain that Jesus is talking about the Holy Spirit, Who He sends to help, comfort, and counsel us. Ask children:

- Imagine walking somewhere blindfolded. How hard would that be?

- What if someone walked beside you to guide you? What difference would that make?

Power Tools

- Blindfold
- Wooden spoon
- 10 cotton balls
- Chair
- 2 bowls

Power Source

"I will ask the Father, and he will give you another *Counselor to be with you forever." John 14:16

*Comforter, kjv; Helper, nkjv

Team-Building Game

Divide into teams of three. Explain that one player should sit in a chair blindfolded with a wooden spoon in his hand and a bowl in his lap filled with 10 cotton balls. He should also have a bowl on his head which is held in place by a teammate. Without help, the seated player should use the wooden spoon to scoop the cotton balls from the bowl in his lap to the bowl on his head.

For the second round, allow the third team member to help. The idea is that it is easier when someone who can see what is happening helps someone who can't. At the end of the game, explain that the Holy Spirit sees the full spiritual situation of whatever we're going through and can help us with God's comfort and counsel.

Power Charge

Review the Power Source verse. Ask children:

- Can you think of ways you might need the Holy Spirit's help? Have you ever asked the Holy Spirit for help, comfort, or counsel (direction)?

Alternate Voltage

To make the game more challenging, play music or have volunteers shout incorrect instructions. Remind children that sometimes we have to hear the Holy Spirit speak to us through the noise in our life.

Hold It Right There!

Energy Level Medium

Starter

This is a game of "try and try again," another way of applying Philippians 3:14: Don't give up. Hang in there and keep pressing on.

Read Philippians 3:14. Ask children:

- Tell about a time when you pressed toward a goal or continued to do something even when you wanted to give up.
- Why is it so easy to get discouraged and want to quit?
- What is the goal that God is calling us to press toward? (On Earth—being more like Jesus; beyond Earth—going to Heaven)

Power Tools

- 2 large toy hoops
- 2–4 beach balls (small enough to be thrown through the hoops)
- Stopwatch

Power Source

"I press on toward the goal to win the prize for which God has called me heavenward in Christ Jesus." Philippians 3:14

Team-Building Game

Divide into two teams. Have two volunteers each hold a hoop. Explain that the two teams will compete against the clock to shoot beach balls through the hoops. For round one, the hoops are stationary. For round two, the hoop holders can move around to challenge the throwers to hit the moving target. The movement can increase in speed. Allow two minutes per round. If children need a challenge, shorten the time.

Power Charge

Review the Power Source verse. Ask children:

- In what ways did this game remind you of Philippians 3:14?
- What kinds of things discourage us from pressing on as Christians?
- Can you put this verse into your own words that apply to your daily life?
- Pretend you are talking to another Christian who is discouraged. What could you say to encourage her to hang in there and keep pressing on for the Lord?

Puppet Power

Starter

In this game, children will make shoe box puppet theaters and perform skits from the Old Testament with their fingers. What we do with our fingers is fun, but it is never as spectacular as what God does with His fingers. This game brings focus to the power and majesty of our Creator God.

Read Job 10:8 and Psalm 8:3–4. Talk about what people do with their hands and fingers. Ask children:

- What creative things can we do with our hands and fingers? (play an instrument, finger paint, make bows, etc.)

- What creations has God made with His hands and fingers?

- How does it make you feel to know that you are the work of His hands?

Power Tools

- Shoe boxes to serve as puppet theaters for teams' performances

- Craft supplies to create backgrounds for the skits and costumes for finger puppets

- Non-toxic, washable markers

Power Source

"When I consider your heavens, the work of your fingers, the moon and the stars which you have set in place, what is man, that you are mindful of him?" Psalm 8:3–4

Team-Building Game

Divide into pairs. Assign each pair an Old Testament story to perform as a short puppet show. Have each pair use craft supplies to create shoe box puppet stages. Let them make costumes for the puppet performers from craft supplies and draw faces on their fingertips with markers. After one team performs, the other team should guess which story was performed. To make the stories more dramatic, add music or lighting.

Power Charge

Review the Power Source verse. Ask children:

- What are some amazing things that God has made in this world?
- What are some amazing things that humans have made in this world?
- What can you make with your hands that will bring glory to God?

Alternate Voltage

Discuss the Puppet Power skits. Encourage children to share positive comments about each performer and the costumes and sets.

Pick a Pair of Parables

Energy Level Medium

Starter

Jesus often taught lessons by telling parables—earthly stories with heavenly meanings. In this mix-and-match game, children will become more familiar with the parables of Christ and learn why Jesus chose to be a storyteller.

Read Matthew 13:34. Ask children:

- What is a parable?

- Why do you think Jesus told stories in His preaching? (It got people's attention; it put His words into pictures that people could relate to and remember)

- What is your favorite parable?

Power Tools

- List of parables (see page 190)
- Chalkboard or white board
- Chalk or markers
- 20 sheets of white drawing paper
- Crayons or colored pencils
- Pencils

Power Source

"Jesus spoke all these things to the crowd in parables; He did not say anything to them without using a parable. Matthew 13:34

Team-Building Game

Write the list of parables in two columns on the board. Briefly explain each story. Divide into two teams. Place each team at a table with drawing supplies and 10 sheets of paper. Have one team choose two parables from the first column and the other team choose two parables from the second column. Instruct each team to illustrate each parable in five scenes (one scene per sheet of paper). Have each team write the parable name and the scene number (1–5) on the back of each sheet. Shuffle each team's 10 pictures. Then, have the teams switch tables. When you say, "Go!," teams should race to put each parable in order. The first team to sequence both parables correctly wins. Have volunteers from each team tell the parable.

Power Charge

Review the Power Source verse. Ask children:

- If you could turn one of Jesus's parables into a movie, which would you choose?
- Pick your favorite parable and tell everyone how it applies to your life.

Alternate Voltage

For a challenge, play the game with additional parables.

What Were You Thinking?

Energy Level

Low

Starter

How amazing! God knows our thoughts, even before we do. When we have good thoughts, He knows them; when we have bad thoughts, He knows them, and He still loves us. This thought-guessing game shows how amazing it is that God knows all of our thoughts.

Read Psalm 139:2. Ask children:

- What does this verse mean to you?
- Have you ever guessed what someone was thinking, just by looking at the expression on his face?
- God knows your thoughts—the good ones and the bad ones. How does that make you feel?

Power Tools

- 10 index cards

Power Source

"You perceive my thoughts from afar." Psalm 139:2

Team-Building Game

Write a Bible-related noun on each index card. Divide into two teams. Have the teams stand in a circle with each team forming half of the circle. Explain that two players should stand in the center—a thought chooser who has the index cards, and a thought keeper. The thought chooser should choose one card and whisper the noun to the thought keeper. (This prevents the thought keeper from changing "thoughts" mid-round.)

Teams should alternate asking thought keeper questions. The thought keeper should give only yes or no answers. Allow each team to ask 10 questions. The team that guesses the thought first wins.

Power Charge

Review the Power Source verse. Ask children:

- Sometimes we think others are thinking bad things about us. How can we be sure that this is so?
- Do you need to think less about certain things and more about other things? Please share some of these.

Alternate Voltage

Play the game against the clock!

First to the Verse

Starter

During this activity, children will realize that it pays to know the Bible. Be having children time how long it takes you to find 2 Timothy 2:15. Before you read it, explain that it's great to know your Bible, and the more you read God's Word, the better you will know it. And the better you know it, the more you'll find God's blessings pouring into your life.

Read 2 Timothy 2:15. Ask children:

- Is there someone you have enjoyed getting to know better by spending more time with him?

- What is the best way to get to know God better?

Power Tools

- 1 Bible per team
- Stopwatch
- Whistle

Power Source

"Do your best to present yourself to God as one approved, a workman who does not need to be ashamed and who correctly handles the word of truth." 2 Timothy 2:15

Team-Building Game

Divide into teams of three. Explain to children that they will race against the clock to find Bible verses. On each team, one player is the page turner. The other two team members coach the page turner, but only the page turner can turn the pages. Tell them that the whistle is the signal to start. The team that finds the most verses wins.

Sample verses: John 3:16; Psalm 23:1; Matthew 6:11; Genesis 12:1; Revelation 1:18; 2 Timothy 2:15

Power Charge

Review the Power Source verse. Ask children:

- The verse talks about a workman who is not ashamed. How does a carpenter, for example, become better at handling his tools?

- How can you become better at handling God's Word?

- Do you have a time each day when you read God's Word? How can you schedule a time and stay faithful to it?

Alternate Voltage

Have the winning team read each verse aloud. Serve a sweet, delicious bread as a snack, reminding children that God's Word is our daily bread. (Matthew 6:11)

Stories 'n' Statues

Starter

What do peanut butter and jelly, soup and sandwich, and faith and works have in common? They all go together. James tells us to show our faith by our works. In this game of statues and Bible stories, children are led to further understand how our works display our faith.

Read James 2:18. Ask children:

- What do you think this verse is saying?
- How do our actions show our faith?
- If we don't show our faith by our actions, what good is our faith to us and others?

Power Tools

- Stopwatch

Power Source

"I will show you my faith by what I do." James 2:18

Team-Building Game

Divide into teams of four. Explain that three team members will perform as statues while the fourth team member directs them. Each team should choose a Bible story to depict in three still scenes. The other teams have one minute to guess the story.

Power Charge

Review the Power Source verse. Ask children:

- How difficult was it to identify Bible stories and characters in only three still scenes?
- Many people will only know us for a short while and will only see a part of our lives. How can we show them the life of Jesus within us?

Alternate Voltage

Allow the statues to speak or move briefly to give helpful clues to the guessing team, then remain still again.

Hot and Cold Blindfold

Energy Level Medium

Starter

People who do not know Christ as their Savior are like those who grope through the darkness. When Christ comes into their lives, He shines His light and makes a difference. This game illustrates the importance of sharing the light of Christ with others.

Read John 8:12. Ask children:

- What do you think it means when someone is walking in darkness?

- Have you ever tried to walk through a dark place when you didn't know the way? What was that like?

- In what ways is walking in darkness similar to how people who do not know the Lord live?

Power Tools

- 2 blindfolds

- Beach balls, basketballs, Bibles, flashlights, unsharpened pencils, paper clips, or other safe objects of various sizes

Power Source

"Jesus spoke again to the people, he said, 'I am the light of the world. Whoever follows me will never walk in darkness, but will have the light of life.'" John 8:12

Team-Building Game

Divide into teams of three. Blindfold one child on each team and have her feel her way around the room, carefully searching for easily identifiable objects like beach balls, as well as hard-to-find objects like paper clips. One team member should hold onto the searcher's arm for safety while the other team member shouts out, "Warm . . . warmer . . . hot . . . red hot!" as the searcher gets closer to the object or "cool . . . cold . . . colder . . . freezing!" as the searcher gets farther from the object. The team that finds the most objects wins.

Power Charge

Review the Power Source verse. Ask children:

- Jesus said, "I am the light of the world." What does this mean for people who don't know Jesus?

- What does it mean when He says that His followers will "never walk in darkness, but will have the light of life"?

- How can you share Jesus with people who do not know Him so that they will have the Light of the world shining in their lives too?

Alternate Voltage

Serve hot chocolate and frozen treats after the game to enjoy something hot and something cold.

One-Armed Sundaes

Energy Level Medium

Starter

Working together can be tons of fun, especially when you're working to make ice-cream sundaes. When each sundae maker has one arm held behind his back, this activity serves as a delicious illustration of working together as the body of Christ.

Read Ephesians 4:16. Have children imagine going through a day with one hand held behind their backs. Ask children:

- What things could you still do with only one hand?

- What things would be difficult to do?

- What does it mean to be part of Christ's body? (The "body" refers to Christ's church, where all members should work together— like parts of our body must work together—to get His work done.)

Power Tools

- Supplies and ingredients to make ice-cream sundaes
- 2 tables
- Stopwatch

Power Source

"From him the whole body, joined and held together by every supporting ligament, grows and builds itself up in love, as each part does its work." Ephesians 4:16

Team-Building Game

Divide into two teams. Explain that each team should work together to make ice-cream sundaes. Teamwork is important, because they are working against the clock, and each player will have a hand held behind her back. Players will have to work together to open a jar of cherries, scoop ice cream, and peel bananas. The first team finished wins. Then, everyone can enjoy the sundaes.

Power Charge

Read the Power Source verse aloud. Ask children:

- How would you put this verse in your own words?
- What can you do, as part of Christ's body, to spread His love and joy in the world?

Alternate Voltage

Record the sundae-making experience. Add music and play the video the next time the group gathers.

Whose Shoes Are Whose?

Energy Level Medium

Starter

In life's decisions, God's wisdom helps us make right choices. This game will demonstrate the value of making good decisions.

Read Proverbs 16:16. Ask children:

- What does it mean to "get wisdom"?

- As Christians, how can we receive God's wisdom into our lives?

Power Tools

- 3–4 extra pairs of shoes

Power Source

"How much better to get wisdom than gold, to choose understanding rather than silver!" Proverbs 16:16

Team-Building Game

Divide into two teams. Have children remove their shoes and place them in a pile. Make sure that pairs are separated. Add a few extra pairs to make it more challenging. Instruct the teams to walk (not run) to the pile, find their shoes, put them on, tie or buckle if needed, and walk (not run) to their seats. The first team to finish wins.

Power Charge

Explain that having wisdom is having the knowledge to make sensible and right decisions and judgments. When we were asked to find our own shoes from all of the others, we needed knowledge of what our shoes looked like in order to make the right choice. We also needed the wisdom to make the right decision to follow the rules when playing the game.

Review the Power Source verse. Ask children:

- Can you think of a time in your life when you did not choose wisely? What happened?

- How can we make wisdom part of our everyday lives—always choosing to seek God's wisdom as easily as choosing our own pair of shoes?

Alternate Voltage

For an added challenge, divide children into pairs. Have each team member find his partner's shoes.

Bible Baseball

Energy Level High

Starter

This game reinforces the concept that knowing and living by God's Word enables us to live freely and helps us stay on the path of His commands. When we rely on God's Word to guide our lives, we can make it to home plate every time!

Read Psalm 119:32 and talk about the different paths people take in life. Remind children that knowing and living by God's Word is always the right path. Ask children:

- Why do you think this Scripture emphasizes running in the path of God's commands?

- How do we "run" the course of God's commandments?

Power Tools

- Tennis balls
- Rubber bands
- Paper and pen
- Baseball mitts for pitchers and catchers
- Bible questions (see page 190)
- White paper cut into strips

Power Source

"I run in the path of your commands, for you have set my heart free."
Psalm 119:32

Outdoor Game

Before the Bible baseball game, review the questions and set the difficulty level for your group. Write each question on a strip of paper. Attach each paper strip to a tennis ball with a rubber band. Find a space to set up the game like a real baseball game with three bases and a home plate. Divide into two teams and assign roles as pitcher and catcher. Have one team take the field and the other line up and get ready to "hit" (answer questions). Explain that team one's pitcher should throw a tennis ball to his catcher who should read the question aloud to team two's first batter. If the batter answers the question correctly, she should run to first base. If the batter does not know the answer, she "strikes out." The game continues according to baseball rules. Play at least three innings (rounds) to be sure that all children get a chance to "bat."

Power Charge

Review the Power Source verse. Ask children:
- When we stray from the path, how do we return?
- How does knowing God's Word help us find success in life?

Anytime Egg Hunt

Energy Level

High

Starter

An egg hunt is fun—and in this game can reinforce Bible knowledge—any time of year.

Read Deuteronomy 4:29 and explain that the word *seek* means *to hunt*. One of the best ways to seek the Lord is to search His Word. We will find blessings and promises waiting there just for us. Ask children:

- When did you hunt for something you really needed to find? How did you feel when you finally found it?
- How do you hunt for, or seek, the Lord in your own life?

Power Tools

- Plastic eggs
- Basket or bag, one per child
- Small bouncy balls (should fit in eggs or bags)
- Small strips of paper with Bible promise references written on them (see page 191)
- Whistle

Power Source

"If from there you seek the Lord your God, you will find him if you look for him with all your heart and with all your soul." Deuteronomy 4:29

Outdoor Game

Place a bouncy ball and Scripture reference in each egg. Have players hold their empty baskets and form a line. Blow the whistle to begin the egg hunt. Once all of the eggs are found, have children open the eggs, read the references, and look in their Bibles for the verses. Have each child read his verses aloud to the class and bounce the ball for every blessing he sees in each verse.

Power Charge

Review the Power Source verse. Ask children:

- What does this Bible verse mean to you?
- Is there someone you know who needs to hear a Bible promise today? What could you say to that person?

Alternate Voltage

For added excitement, use a timer and have the players race against the clock to find all of the eggs. After discussion, have a contest to see who can dribble the bouncy ball the most times in a row.

Hop Counters

Energy Level High

Starter

This game demonstrates how amazing God is and points out how much He loves us.

Read Matthew 10:30. Ask children:

- What are some things on Earth that are impossible for humans to count?
- Do you think that God could count all of these things?

Power Tools

- Striped or colorful shirts to designate Count Coaches (should be teens or older)
- Strips of fabric (to safely bind together children's legs for the three-legged race)
- Whistle
- Crepe paper
- Masking tape

Power Source

"Even the very hairs of your head are all numbered." Matthew 10:30

Outdoor Game

Divide into pairs. Have several pairs line up at the starting line (marked with masking tape). Safely and comfortably bind together one leg from each child. Explain that as they hop together to the finish line (marked with crepe paper), each pair should silently count how many hops it takes them. A Count Coach should follow beside each pair to take a more accurate count. Allow spectators to whistle and cheer to make it more difficult for each pair to count their hops.

Power Charge

Review the Power Source verse. Ask children:

- How far off was your hop count from the Count Coach's count? Was it difficult to count?
- Why is it important that God knows the number of hairs on your head? What other things do you think God has "numbered?"

Alternate Voltage

Once the hoppers get the hang of it, create a few obstacles on the course. Let the Count Coaches take a break while the children hop around on the "Hip-Hopstacle Course."

Beach Ball Seven-Up

Energy Level
High

Starter

This beach ball bouncing game serves as a reminder to praise God at least seven times a day. Once a praise habit is formed, it can lead to a fountainhead of blessings!

Read Psalm 119:164. Ask children:

- How do you feel when somebody praises you?

- The writer of this Psalm is encouraging us to praise the Lord more than once or twice a week. What are ways that we can praise Him more often?

Power Tools

- 3 or 4 beach balls (or more if desired)

Power Source

"Seven times a day I praise you."
Psalm 119:164

Outdoor Game

Begin by allowing each child to pat or bump a beach ball into the air seven times consecutively. (Three or four players can do this at the same time.) Then, multiply the number and have two players work together to attempt 14 hits, have three players attempt 21 hits, etc. The game can also be played with a volleyball net. In this version, two teams play against each other. Each team should hit the beach ball seven, 14, or 21 times before passing it over the net to the other team. As players keep the beach balls in the air, have them shout praises to God.

Power Charge

Review the Power Source verse. Ask children:

- Was it easy or difficult to keep the beach ball in the air?

- Did you notice that the more you played, the easier it was to get the feel of hitting the ball?

- What are some habits of praise that we could develop in our lives?

Alternate Voltage

Challenge children to praise the Lord seven times each day during the coming week. Follow up the next week to see how they did.

Stand Up, Sit Down Challenge

Energy Level Medium

Starter

As children enjoy a blindfolded guessing game, they will also learn the amazing truth that God knows our thoughts—each and every one.

Read Psalm 139:2. Ask children:

- How does it make you feel to know that God knows your every thought and your every action?

Power Tools

- 1 blindfold per team

Power Source

"You know when I sit and when I rise; you perceive my thoughts from afar." Psalm 139:2

Outdoor Game

Divide into equal teams. Each team should play their own game. Explain that on each team, one child should be blindfolded. The team members should stand shoulder to shoulder, forming a line. The blindfolded child should take three big steps forward and start the game by saying, "Stand up. Sit down. Go!" Staying in place, the row of players should randomly arrange themselves as standers or sitters. After a few seconds, the blindfolded player should guess how many are standing and how many are sitting. Play several times, allowing the children to change roles.

Power Charge

Review the Power Source verse. Ask children:

- There is nothing we can hide from God. He knows our every move and every thought—even before we do or say anything. How should this affect your daily life?

Alternate Voltage

For an added challenge, have the blindfolded player guess the order of the standers and sitters. (For example, from left to right, Andrew standing, Loren sitting, Alex sitting, etc.)

Touchdown Quiz

Energy Level
Medium

Starter

This game demonstrates the principle that knowing God's Word and living by His commands gives us the strength to "press on" in life. The Christian life can be like a game of football—in our walk with the Lord, we sometimes move forward, but sometimes we move backward as well—just like a team on the football field. The key is to never give up!

Read Philippians 3:14. Ask children:

- What things in our life help move us forward with the Lord? What things can move us away from Him?

- In what ways can we "press on toward the goal" in our Christian lives?

Power Tools

- Goal markers, one for each end of the field (poles, stakes, or end zone markers that can be seen from across the field)

- Bible quiz questions (see page 191)

- Coin for coin toss

Power Source

"I press on toward the goal to win the prize for which God has called me heavenward in Christ Jesus." Philippians 3:14

Outdoor Game

Divide into two teams. Have both teams form a line at the midpoint of the field, facing each other. Toss a coin to determine which team will answer the first Bible question. Every time a player answers correctly, the team moves one step toward their goal. This drives the opposing team backward, away from their goal. If the team answers incorrectly, they should take a step backward. The first team to the end zone wins.

Power Charge

Review the Power Source verse. Toss a foam football to each child as she answers a question. Ask children:

- What does today's Bible verse mean to you?

- This week, how can you "press toward the goal" to know Christ better?

- When we make mistakes, or do bad things, we lose yardage in our Christian lives. What can we do to start moving forward again?

Alternate Voltage

For older children, add fill-in-the-blank Bible quiz questions with increased difficulty.

I Flee from Thee

Energy Level
High

Starter

Hide-and-Seek is a game that we can never play with God. He always knows where we are hiding, even before we get there. We can play it with each other and learn more about the loving Lord Jesus who always seeks to enjoy our friendship.

Read Psalm 139:7. Ask children:

- What was the best hiding place you've ever found?
- Some people do bad things and hope that God doesn't know about them. What does today's verse say about that idea?

Power Tools

- Stopwatch

Power Source

"Where can I go from Your Spirit? Where can I flee from Your presence?" Psalm 139:7

Outdoor Game

Explain that in this game of Hide-and-Seek, the hiders have one or two minutes (depending on the size of the area) to find their hiding places. Identify what areas are out-of-bounds before the game begins. Establish a home base where the hiders should return before the seeker tags them. Whenever the seeker wants, she can yell, "I find thee!" All of the hiders should answer, "I flee thee!" and, if they want to, run toward home base. Periodically, designate a new seeker.

Power Charge

Review the Power Source verse. Ask children:

- When you were a hider, did you think your hiding place would keep you hidden for a long time? Why or why not?
- In this Scripture passage, it sounds like the author wants to "flee" from God. Have you ever felt like fleeing and hiding because of something you did?
- How does knowing that you cannot hide anything from God change the way you approach God in your prayer? How does it change the way you act in your daily life?

Alternate Voltage

If possible and safe, play the game at night with flashlights. Remind children not to shine the flashlights toward anyone's face. This would be a great game for an overnight retreat!

Doughnut Drill

Energy Level

High

Starter

This game demonstrates the importance of prompt obedience.

Read Ephesians 6:1–3. Ask children:

- What does it mean to obey?
- When is it easy for you to obey your parents, and when is it not so easy?
- Why is it important to learn obedience, not just at home, but as we grow into adults?

Power Tools

- 2 inflatable round pool toys, large enough for a child to squeeze through

Power Source

"Children, obey your parents in the Lord, for this is right. 'Honor your father and mother'—which is the first commandment with a promise— 'that it may go well with you and that you may enjoy long life on the earth.'"
Ephesians 6:1–3

Outdoor Game

Divide into two teams. Have each team form a single-file line. Explain that the pool toy or "doughnut" should start at the head of each line. The first player should pull the doughnut over his head, his body, and his feet, and step out of it to pass it to the player behind him. She should step into it and pull it over her body and head and pass it to the player behind her, etc. Teams should race to see which will pass their doughnut through the line and back to win. Explain that throughout the game, you will yell, "Freeze!" and teams should obey immediately and hold their poses until you unfreeze them by saying, "Go!"

Power Charge

Have children sit with their teams and discuss:

- Was it difficult to obey when you heard the "Freeze!" command?
- How did it feel to hold the frozen pose when you were eager to get the game going again?
- God's Word tells us that obedience actually comes with a promise. What is that promise? What does that mean?
- In what ways can you make a new commitment to obey your parents?

Alternate Voltage

During the game, shout commands that the players have to "obey" as they are playing, such as: Sing Row, Row, Row Your Boat aloud, use only one hand, hop on one foot, etc.

I Gotcha!

Energy Level **High**

Starter

This game reminds children that they must stay far away from sin.

Read James 4:7–8. Open the discussion by stating that we all want to resist the devil, resist sinful ways, and draw near to God. But sometimes, we don't resist temptation and draw close to sin instead of to God. This verse tells us that if we resist, the temptation will disappear. Ask children:

- How does the devil try to move us away from God and closer to his sinful ways?
- How can we resist the devil's ways?
- Can you think of ways that you are tempted to do wrong things?

Power Tools

- None

Power Source

"Submit yourselves, then, to God. Resist the devil, and he will flee from you. Come near to God and He will come near to you." James 4:7–8

Outdoor Game

Have the children form a line against a wall, or safety zone. Designate one child as Mr. (or Ms.) Supposer and have him stand far away from the group. Explain that the children should call out, "Mr. Supposer, can we come closer?" He should reply, "I suppose. Ten steps closer!" They should take 10 steps toward him. This continues until, at some point, Mr. Supposer yells, "I gotcha!" and runs to tag as many of them as he can before they reach the safety zone. Each tagged player joins Mr. Supposer to tag the remaining children. Play until all children are tagged.

Power Charge

Review the Power Source verse. Ask children to form several teams to create skits about Christians who are tempted to sin and try to resist. Teams can make them humorous. For example, the sin is eating dozens of doughnuts at once, stealing the world's biggest candy bar, or telling a fantastic lie to a teacher. They should show the Christian giving into temptation in one skit and resisting in the next version. Then, ask children:

- How can submitting to God, and staying close to Him, help us resist the devil?

Alternate Voltage

Have Ms. Supposer give marching orders rather than numbers of steps to be taken. Children should march closer to Ms. Supposer until told to halt.

Freeze and Unfreeze

Energy Level High

Starter

This tag game shows what happens when parts of our bodies stop doing their jobs. More importantly, it shows the value of each member in the Body of Christ.

Read 1 Corinthians 12:27 and then 1 Corinthians 12:18–21. Explain that each of us is a valuable part of the Body of Christ. We may not feel like we're that important, but God's Word tells us that He can't do His work here on Earth without His body! That's us!

Power Tools

- None

Power Source

"Now you are the body of Christ, and each one of you is a part of it."
1 Corinthians 12:27

Outdoor Game

Designate two children to be Freezers and two to be Unfreezers. The rest of the group should be the Chosen-to-Be-Frozen. Explain that when Freezers tag a "Chosen" child, the place where they tag them becomes frozen. Freezers may only tag arms or legs. A Freezer can only tag one child in one place. Then, the freezer should move to the next child. The Chosen children try to stay away from the Freezers, but they should get progressively more frozen until an Unfreezer unfreezes them. An Unfreezer can only "unfreeze" one arm or leg at a time. Play until all children are frozen. Then, have children thaw, switch roles, and play again.

Power Charge

Review the Power Source verse. Ask children:

- What happened when a leg or arm was "frozen"?
- What part do you think you play in doing God's work?
- If you want to convince a friend that she is important to God and His work, what would you say?

Alternate Voltage

Have children talk about their own and others' special gifts and contributions to the Body of Christ.

Follow Christ's Example

Do What I Do

Energy Level

High

Starter

Being a Christian is just being a follower of Christ—simple, but not easy. In this game of echoing movements, children will learn how much work it takes to duplicate someone's actions.

Read Matthew 9:9. Ask children:

- When Jesus asked Matthew to follow Him, do you think that Matthew knew what adventures were ahead of him?
- What were some big adventures in the life and ministry of Christ?

Power Tools

- Parking lot cones, flags, or something to clearly mark point A and point B

Power Source

"'Follow me,' he told him, and Matthew got up and followed him." Matthew 9:9

Outdoor Game

Designate point A about 10 feet (3 meters) away from Point B. Have children form a single-file line behind point A. Explain that the first child will take a funny walk-stroll from point A to point B. The next child should duplicate that walk. Encourage children to take one or two hops, a spin, a frog leap, a crab walk, anything that the next player has to remember and follow. Encourage them to increase the complexity of their actions as the game continues.

Power Charge

Review the Power Source verse. Ask children:

- Is it easy or difficult to follow Christ?
- How do we follow Him, when He's not physically on Earth anymore?
- Matthew left his tax collecting business to follow Jesus. Are there some things in your life that you might need to leave behind to be a more faithful follower of your Lord?
- Who are some people in your life whose words and ways remind you of Christ?

Alternate Voltage

Let players take turns doing the same thing, but increase the distance between A and B, or use a timer to play against the clock.

Calling All Creatures

Starter

All creation is called to praise the Lord. That is a lot of praising from a lot of creatures—all the way from creepy crawlers to feathered flyers to prancing princes to elderly elders. During this game, children will learn about all of this wonderful praising.

Read Psalm 148:7, 10–12. Ask children:

- Why did God make so many different creatures to praise Him?
- How can we join the praises of creation?

Power Tools

- Crepe paper
- Music CD
- CD player
- A metal bucket and spoon
- Microphone, megaphone, or shout-funnel

Power Source

"Praise the Lord from the earth . . . . wild animals and all cattle, small creatures and flying birds, kings of the earth and all nations, you princes and all rulers on earth, young men and maidens, old men and children." Psalm 148:7, 10–12

Outdoor Game

Mark a finish line with colorful crepe paper. Divide into two or three teams. Let children race to see which team can get to the finish line first. Explain that to get there, players must imitate the creatures explained and implied in Psalm 148:7 10–12. Start the music and use the microphone to announce, "Tigers and lions, ready, set . . ." Then, hit the metal bucket to start the creatures "praising the Lord" across the open area toward the finish line. Explain that when you hit the bucket again, they should freeze, waiting for your next creature call. Have players imitate flying birds, princes, bugs, even babies, all praising the Lord. Teams will wiggle, gallop, leap, and crawl their way to victory.

Power Charge

Review the Power Source verse. Ask children:

- The last verse of the Psalm tells us to praise the Lord. How do you praise the Lord?
- How do you think that God feels when He gets praise from the birds and bugs? How does that compare to when He receives praise from us?

Alternate Voltage

Have someone videotape the activity and watch it as a group.

Team Walk

Energy Level Medium

Starter

It is our job to show the world that we are united in the love of our Lord. This game demonstrates that we all need to get along and cooperate with each other.

Discuss some obvious ways that God made each of us different: eye color, hair color, likes and dislikes, talents, etc. Point out that we are all different in a variety of ways, yet Jesus Christ asks us to come together as His disciples and to show His love to one another.

Read John 13:35. Ask children:

- What prevents us from getting along?
- What do we need to be the kind of disciples Jesus wants?

Power Tools

- Long pieces of thick, soft rope or strong fabric (to wrap safely and comfortably around the children)
- Flags or colorful fabric on poles (for the starting and finish lines)

Power Source

"By this all men will know that you are my disciples, if you love one another." John 13:35

Outdoor Game

Have extra adults a help enforce safety during this game. Arranged by size or age and gender, gather 10 children together into a tight bunch. Carefully bind together the children with soft rope or fabric and prepare them to move forward together. Explain that they should move slowly, especially at first, so that no one gets yanked or pushed. There should be some jostling, but that's what makes it fun. Have each team walk slowly from the starting line to the finish line, acting as a team. Repeat the game until all children have had a turn.

Power Charge

Review the Power Source verse. Ask children:

- How did the teams begin? Were they very good at walking?
- How did they look as the game progressed?
- How can we work together, get along better, and be more like the disciples of our Lord?

Alternate Voltage

Try some Team Olympics. Have groups compete by performing a smooth, graceful complete turn-around or three well-coordinated hops.

Over and Under

Energy Level Medium

Starter

This game provides a fun lesson in perseverance.

Read James 1:12. Ask children:

- What does the word *perseverance* mean to you?
- What is this verse telling us?

Power Tools

- Whistle
- Several rolls of bath tissue
- 2 small plastic garbage bags

Power Source

"Blessed is the man who perseveres under trial, because when he has stood the test, he will receive the crown of life that God has promised to those who love him." James 1:12

Outdoor Game

Divide into two teams. Have teams stand about 10 feet (3 meters) apart, each in a single-file line. Give a roll of bath tissue to the first person in each line. Explain that when the signal is given, the first player on each team should pass the bath tissue backward by passing it over his head and holding onto the first sheet on the roll. The roll should travel to the back of the line. The roll should then be passed to the front between players' feet. Each time the tissue tears, the team should start again. If the tissue does not tear, the team should continue until the roll is empty. To end the game, have each team race to gather all of the bath tissue and deposit it in their garbage bag.

Power Charge

As a group, recite the Power Source verse three times. Ask for three children to put the verse into their own words. Break into small groups and discuss:

- What does the Bible mean by those who have "stood the test"?
- Do you know someone who is taking a brave stand through a difficult trial?

Alternate Voltage

For a challenge, have the teams complete the game blindfolded.

String Stompers

Energy Level High

Starter

In this game, children will learn more about Jesus' sacrifice on the cross.
Read John 1:29. Ask children:

- If you were to write a thank-you card to Jesus for taking away your sin, what would you say?

Power Tools

- 18" (45 cm) length of red yarn, one per child
- A garbage can with a sign attached:
  MY SIN: Forgiven and Forgotten! John 1:29
- White string (to mark the playing field)

Power Source

"The next day John saw Jesus coming toward him and said, 'Look, the Lamb of God, who takes away the sin of the world!'" John 1:29

Outdoor Game

Provide each child with a length of red yarn and instruct him to tuck it into the back of one shoe so that it stays in place while he is running. Have him leave enough yarn hanging out of the shoe so that the string can be stomped on and pulled out by another player. Explain that when the game starts, children should chase each other and stomp strings in order to pull them out. When a player stomps on another player's string and it pulls free, she should yell, "Your sin is gone!" That player takes his string and deposits it in the garbage can.

Power Charge

Review the Power Source verse. Ask children:
- Why is Jesus called "the Lamb of God"?
- Have you received forgiveness and freedom from your sin?

Alternate Voltage

After the players put their red strings in the garbage can, provide each child with a small bottle of bubbles to blow as a symbol of being free from their sin.

One Word at a Time

Energy Level Medium

Starter

What a joy it is to know that children can have a personal relationship with Jesus Christ. This sentence completion game about what Christ means to them will help children verbalize their devotion to the Lord and have fun doing it.

Read John 21:15–17. Explain that Jesus wanted to know if Simon Peter loved Him more than anything and anyone. He even asked him that question three times! Ask children:

- Who are the people in your family who tell you that they love you? How and when do they tell you that they love you?
- What would you say to Jesus if He asked you if you truly love Him?

Power Tools

- 7 or 8 balls of different types and sizes
- Music CD
- CD player

Power Source

"Jesus said to Simon Peter, 'Simon, son of John, do you truly love me more than these?'" John 21:15

Outdoor Game

Prepare children for meaningful sentence-making by creating silly sentences together. Give each child a simple sentence starter, such as "I love . . . " Allow children to complete the sentences. Have children create sentences one person/one word at a time. When they understand the concept, begin the game by having children stand in a circle, shoulder to shoulder. Distribute the balls randomly. When the music starts, the balls should be passed from person to person (slowly for a slow song and quickly for a fast song). When the music pauses, everyone stops. Together, the children holding the balls should complete a spontaneous meaningful sentence. Have them begin with "Jesus is . . ." Remember to occasionally switch directions during play.

Power Charge

Go to a different location for discussion and play children's worship music. Ask children:

- How do we show Jesus that you love Him?
- Have you ever expressed your love to Him in worship or in prayer?

Alternate Voltage

Additional suggestions for sentence starters are:

I will show my love by . . .

I praise Him for . . .

Jug Toss Challenge

Energy Level Medium

Starter

In John 15, Jesus says that we are like branches attached to a vine. He is calling us to live a life attached to Him, never separated, always close. This tossing game illustrates the truth that life is better living close to Jesus.

Read John 15:4. Explain that remaining, or abiding, means staying so close that you receive your life from the vine. Jesus wants us to stay that close to Him, receiving our joy and strength and peace from Him. Ask children:

- How do we stay close to Christ throughout the day?

- When we stay close to Christ, He says we bear fruit. What kind of fruit is He talking about?

Power Tools

- 2 plastic gallon milk jugs
- Masking tape
- Tennis ball
- Scissors

Power Source

"Remain in me, and I will remain in you." John 15:4

Outdoor Game

Make jug catchers by cutting the top portion from each milk jug, leaving the handles intact. Cover the cut edges with masking tape for safety. Divide players into pairs. Each pair should stand facing each other, jug catchers in hand; one should have the tennis ball. Pairs begin very close to each another so that it is not a challenge to throw the tennis ball into the other person's jug catcher. After each throw, have them take one step away from each other. Have children see how far apart they can get and still throw the ball into their partner's jug catcher. Have the other children cheer for and encourage the players.

Power Charge

Remind children that we know that whether or not we feel close to Christ, when we move close to Him, He will move close to us. "Come near to God and He will come near to you." (James 4:8) Explain what you do to come near to God. Review the Power Source verse. Ask children:

- Can you think of a time you felt very close to the Lord? What happened?

- Can you think of a time when you felt like He was a million miles away?

Alternate Voltage

For a challenge, use small, half-filled water balloons instead of tennis balls.

Beach Ball Bowling

Energy
Level
Medium

Starter

Paul's words in 1 Thessalonians urge us to live in constant communication with God. When we've prayed for something according to God's Word, we can continue to thank Him for the answer even before we receive it. This kind of faithful persistence will also help children as they try to knock over human bowling pins.

Read 1 Thessalonians 5:17. Discuss prayer as something we do continually rather than once or twice. Ask children:

- Have you ever had to do something that took a long time and was much harder than you expected?

- Tell about a time you almost quit. Explain why you did not quit, even while enduring frustration.

Power Tools

- Several beach balls
- Several rolls of bath tissue

Power Source

"Pray continually."
1 Thessalonians 5:17

Outdoor Game

Divide into two teams. Depending on the size of your class, have some children volunteer to be bowling pins and a few volunteer to be bowlers. Have children carefully wrap the "pins" in bath tissue from ankles to necks. Explain that the bowlers should kneel with their hands behind their backs and nudge the beach ball toward the "pins" with their noses. Once the ball touches a "pin," that person cannot hit another pin. The team to knock all of the "pins" down first wins.

Power Charge

Review the Power Source verse. Ask children:

- Was there a time in your life when you were really praying for something? Was your prayer answered in the way you thought it would be?

- What discourages us from praying?

- Do you have a need that we can all pray about?

All Talk and No Walk

Energy Level **Medium**

Starter

This Bible character charades game demonstrates the two parts of faith, showing children the importance of the walk and the talk of Christian life.

Read James 2:17–18. Explain that our faith has two parts: what we believe, and how our actions show others what we believe. Faith is only complete when both parts are actively working. Ask children:

- Can you put the Bible verse in your own words?
- What are the most important ways a Christian shows others that he is a Christian?

Power Tools

- None

Power Source

"Faith by itself, if it is not accompanied by action, is dead. I will show you my faith by what I do." James 2:17–18

Outdoor Game

Divide into two teams. Explain that each team selects an actor to portray a Bible character. The actor should focus on how the character walks—no talking or sound effects. The other team should try to guess which character is being portrayed. If necessary, the actor's team may provide two clues. If the Bible character is not guessed, in round two, the actor may talk and walk. Everyone will quickly discover that it is much easier to tell what is happening when they see and hear the walk and the talk.

Power Charge

Review the Power Source verse. Ask children:

- What do you think it means to have faith? (Read Hebrews 11:1 for a biblical definition.)
- How can you show your faith to others who don't share your faith in Christ?

Alternate Voltage

Discuss how each character impacted those around him with his walk and talk.

Word Line

Energy Level Medium

Starter

In this word-guessing game, children try to put the words of a Scripture verse in order. They will need to separate the "good" words from words that don't belong. God knows what we will say—good or bad. We should strive to speak only good things, and throw away the words in our life that "don't belong."

Read Psalm 139:4. Talk about how amazing it is that God knows our words before we ever say them. Ask children:

- Have you ever had someone in your life tell you "I know what you are going to say"? Did that person really know what you were going to say?

- What can we do to make sure our words are always "good" and please God?

Power Tools

- 4 chairs (2 per team)
- 6' (2 m) of string per team
- 35–40 index cards
- 20–30 clip clothespins

Power Source

"Before a word is on my tongue you know it completely, O Lord." Psalm 139:4

Outdoor Game

Divide into two teams. Create two sets of index cards by writing Psalm 139:4, one word per card. For a challenge, write some words that do not belong in the verse. Create a "Word Line", similar to a clothesline, with the string and two chairs placed several feet (1–2 meters) away from each team. Place 10–15 clothespins on the ground in front of the chairs. Place the index cards facedown in front of each team. Explain that at your signal, players should choose a card, race to the Word Line, and using a clothespin, clip the word on the string as it appears in the Scripture verse. If the word does not belong, the player leaves the card on the ground, and returns to her team. The next player may choose a new card and clip it in place on the Word Line, move a word already on the Word Line to another position, or remove a word from the Word Line that doesn't belong. The team that arranges the Scripture words in the correct order wins.

Power Charge

Review the Power Source verse. Explain that God knows us completely and His love never ends. He knows the words of our hearts, as well as the words that we speak. Ask children:

- Was it difficult to decide if a word belonged on the Word Line? Is it always easy to choose the right words to speak?

Alternate Voltage

For younger players, clip several words in place on the Word Line before the children play the game.

Crazy Carrier

Starter

We may not always be called to physically carry each other, but God calls us to carry each others burdens, or troubles, as if they were our own. As the children participate in this game, it will remind them that there will be times when they will need to be "carried" through some tough times, and other times, they will have to carry others—without complaining.

Read Galatians 6:2. Comment that in the same way that our game will be silent, our actions will speak louder than words when we help our brothers and sisters in Christ. Ask children:

- What does it mean to "carry" other's burdens?

Power Tools

- Blankets (one per team)
- Masking tape
- Chairs (one per team)

Power Source

Carry each other's burdens, and in this way you will fulfill the law of Christ. Galatians 6:2

Silent Game

Divide into equal teams of at least five players. Remind children that this is a silent game. Give each team a blanket and have them form a line at the starting line (marked with masking tape). Place a chair several feet (2–3 meters) in front of each team. Place the blankets on the floor and ask the first player from each team to sit in the middle of the blanket. The other four players should grab the four corners of the blanket. Each team should gently pull each player around the chair and back to the starting line. The player who was seated becomes a carrier. The next player then sits on the blanket to be carried. Repeat until all players on each team have been carried and a carrier.

Power Charge

Review the Power Source verse. Ask children:

- How did our game reflect God's command of "carrying each other's burdens"?
- What can we do to "carry" each others' burdens?

Alternate Voltage

Have players carry two players at a time.

Bible Book Boogie

Energy Level Medium

Starter

This game encourages children to learn the books of the Bible.

Read Joshua 1:7. Remind children that these words were spoken by God Himself to Joshua. After 40 years of wandering in the wilderness, the Israelites were finally crossing the Jordan River into the Promised Land. God knew there would be battles against others for the land, as well as struggles among his people to keep His commands. These encouraging words, to carefully and consistently obey God's Word, come with a promise. Ask children:

- How would you have felt hearing these instructions from God?

- What does the Scripture mean when it says, "Do not turn from it to the right or to the left"?

- How can knowing and obeying God's commands make us strong and courageous?

Power Tools

- 132 index cards

- Stopwatch

- Two tables with enough space to place the index cards in order

Power Source

"Be strong and very courageous. Be careful to obey all the law my servant Moses gave you; do not turn from it to the right or to the left, that you may be successful wherever you go." Joshua 1:7

Silent Game

Depending on the Bible knowledge of your group, you may want to teach them the order of the Bible books in advance, so that each team member will be able to contribute to the game. Print the names of the 66 books of the Bible on two sets of index cards. Divide into two teams. Shuffle the index cards and place each set facedown on a table. Gather the teams around the table. Explain that while working against the clock, children should turn over the cards and put them in order. Begin with the books of the Old Testament, then the New Testament, then all of the books for one final challenge round!

Power Charge

Review the Power Source verse. Ask children:

- What are your dreams and plans for the future? How will obeying God's Word help you?

Alternate Voltage

Allow each team to use a Bible to help them three times during the game.

Linked in Love

Starter

In this game, children link elbows and duplicate each other's movements. It illustrates the concept that we follow Christ not just as single followers, but as many followers linked together.

Read Philippians 3:17. Ask children:

- What does the writer, Paul the Apostle, mean when he asks other Christians to follow his example?
- Paul tells Christians to follow those who live Christ-like lives. Do you imitate the examples of Christ-following people? Who are they?
- What is the "pattern" that Paul is talking about?

Power Tools

- None

Power Source

"Join with others in following my example, brothers, and take note of those who live according to the pattern we gave you."
Philippians 3:17

Silent Game

Divide into pairs. Explain that during this game, two children link elbows. Another pair of children do the same thing. The first pair makes a series of distinct actions (for example, three hops forward, one complete spin, two bows forward, and a jump). Then, the second pair should duplicate the first pair's movements.

Power Charge

Review the Power Source verse. Ask children:

- What models has God placed in your life?
- Can you think of Bible characters whose lives we can follow?
- Can you think of people from the Bible whose lives we should not imitate?
- How can you make your life a Christ-like model for others to follow?

Alternate Voltage

Create excitement by making the movements more complicated and increasing the teams to three or four people.

Really Loud 'n' Silent

Energy Level

Low

Starter

This silent game challenges children to express emotions through movement alone. Through emotions, God comes to us, bringing joy for the sad times and hope when things seem to be hopeless.

Read Psalm 42:11. Ask children:

- Have you ever felt that your soul was downcast (very sad)? How did you change your mood?
- What other emotions do we feel?

Power Tools

- Whiteboard or chalkboard
- Markers or chalk

Power Source

"Why are you downcast, O my soul? Why so disturbed within me? Put your hope in God." Psalm 42:11

Silent Game

Explain that like in charades, one or two children will perform an emotion using only movement and expressions. To keep the game completely silent, write a list of emotions on the board. To guess, a child should raise her hand and wait to be called on. The child should silently approach the list and point to the emotion that she is guessing. If her guess is correct, she should cross out or erase the word from the list, then take a turn performing an emotion.

Power Charge

Talk about the silent skits. Review the Power Source verse. Ask children:

- What did it feel like to show emotions without talking? Was it easy or difficult?
- What are some things you can do if you are feeling downcast?
- If you were to write a letter to someone going through a tough time and wanted to encourage him to "put his hope in God," what would you say?

Alternate Voltage

Have each child write a letter of encouragement to someone and include Psalm 42:11.

Freeze Me, Free You

Starter

We live in a "me"-oriented world. Many things around us, from television and magazines to the Internet, tell us to focus on taking care of ourselves. Yet, God calls us to put others above ourselves by being devoted—committed and loyal—to each other. In this game, children tag their frozen friends, setting them free, illustrating the freeing power of "others"-oriented living.

Read Romans 12:10. Ask children:

- In your opinion, do people think more about themselves or about others?

- What does our Bible verse say to you about this?

Power Tools

- Name tags

Power Source

"Be devoted to one another in brotherly love. Honor one another above yourselves." Romans 12:10

Silent Game

Appoint several children to be Mr. (or Ms.) FreezeYa. Give them name tags. The other children should be in two groups: players who can be frozen and players who can unfreeze others. Explain that the FreezeYa players will walk around and tag players. When players are tagged, they should hold out their arms and freeze. If an unfrozen player walks under the outstretched arms of a frozen player, the frozen player becomes unfrozen. Play until everyone is frozen, then let others be Mr. and Ms. FreezeYa.

Power Charge

Review the Power Source verse. Ask children

- When you were playing this game, did you find yourself focusing on your "frozen" teammates above yourself? How did it feel to free them so they could play?

- How can we become more devoted to others?

- What are some of the practical ways that we can show what the Bible calls "brotherly love" to each other?

Alternate Voltage

Have children draw pictures of themselves putting the needs of others above their own.

Silent Fruit Scramble

Energy Level Medium

Starter

This game sends children scrambling to find others who share their favorite fruits. It also encourages children to bear fruit for Christ.

Read John 15:5-8. Ask children:

• What does a tree or plant need to grow and bear fruit? How do you know if a tree or plant is well cared for?

• What does the Bible mean when it calls us to bear fruit?

• As a Christian, what kind of fruit should you bear? (Read Galatians 5:22.)

Power Tools

• Stopwatch

Power Source

"This is to my Father's glory, that you bear much fruit, showing yourselves to be my disciples." John 15:8

Silent Game

Explain to children that they should silently organize themselves in groups according to their favorite fruit. Tell them that they can form the names of the fruit with their lips (silently), use their hands to describe the fruits, or even pantomime. Give children one minute to organize by favorite fruits. Once they can speak again, have the children discuss whether they completed the task successfully.

Power Charge

Review the Power Source verse. Ask children:

• How does bearing fruit show others that we are Christ's disciples?

• How does our fruit bearing bring glory to God?

• What can you do this week to bear fruit that will bless your family, your friends, and your teachers?

Alternate Voltage

Let children create a skit about two trees, one fruit-bearing and one barren. Have them show what the barren tree did in order to bear fruit, and how it felt one spring when her branches were finally filled with delicious fruit. Perform the skit for a younger class.

Truth Twisters

Energy Level Low

Starter

This simple silent game illustrates how truth is easily distorted when passed from one person to another. It is a fun game that will impart a serious message to young believers.

Read Ephesians 4:29. Ask children:

- What does the Bible mean by "building up others"?
- What kind of words build us up? What kind of words tear us down?

Power Tools

- Paper and pencils

Power Source

"Do not let any unwholesome talk come out of your mouths, but only what is helpful for building others up according to their needs, that it may benefit those who listen." Ephesians 4:29

Silent Game

Divide into two teams. Have each team form a side-by-side line, facing the other team. Choose a line leader for each team. Whisper a different message clearly into the ear of each line leader. Each line leader should return to her line and whisper that message to the next person in line, making sure that no one else in the line can hear it. The last person in each line should write the message he has heard and read it to the group. By the time it has passed from person to person, the message usually makes no sense. Finally, have each line leader say the original messages. Play at least two rounds.

Sample Messages: My brother's uncle likes to keep monkeys in his backyard. I wanted to ride my bicycle, but the front tire was flat.

Power Charge

Review the Power Source verse. Ask children:

- By the time the message made it to the end of the line, was it something that would "benefit those who listened"?
- What are some examples of "unwholesome talk"?
- How can we avoid this negative type of talk?

Alternate Voltage

Play the game with longer messages. The longer the message, the more bizarre it will become as it travels from person to person.

Craft Stick Charades

Energy Level Low

Starter

God uses many messengers to tell His story. Job made a list of unlikely Bible teachers: animals, birds, Earth, and fish. This activity will have children telling each other about the greatness of God through craft stick charades.

Read Job 12:7–8. Explain that in this Bible story, Job was telling his not-so-friendly friends that God was in charge, even though Job was experiencing major trials in his life. If they didn't believe that He held power over all things, Job said that the animals, birds, fish, and the entire Earth were explaining God's rulership.
Ask children:

- How can animals and the earth explain God's power, since they can't talk?

Power Tools

- Wooden craft sticks
- Craft supplies
- Glue
- Tables, one per team

Power Source

"Ask the animals, and they will teach you, or the birds of the air, and they will tell you; or speak to the earth, and it will teach you, or let the fish of the sea inform you."
Job 12:7–8

Silent Game

Divide into several teams. Instruct each team to sit at a table to make simple wooden craft stick puppets, props, and backdrops if needed. Then, have children perform silent puppet shows to teach each other about God's greatness and power as demonstrated through well-known Bible stories. Remind teams to work quietly to keep their projects secret. Have the teams guess the stories being performed and what each story teaches about God.

Power Charge

Review the Power Source verse. Ask children:

- When you look at the wonders of the world and the beautiful animals in creation, what does it make you think about God?
- How can we share the message of God's love and power without words?

Alternate Voltage

Add drama by darkening the room and using flashlights to light the puppet shows. Remind students not to shine flashlights toward anyone's face.

Spoon to Spoon to Spoon

Energy Level **Medium**

Starter

This silent game requires precise movements against the clock—a fun way to illustrate our need to grow in patience.

Read 1 Thessalonians 5:14. Ask children:

- Can you think of something that really tries your patience?

- When was the last time you had to patiently wait for something?

- Why does God want us to develop patience?

Power Tools

- Plastic spoons

- Small, individually-wrapped hard candies

- Masking tape

Power Source

"Be patient with everyone."
1 Thessalonians 5:14

Silent Game

Divide into two teams. Have each team line up single file behind the starting line (marked with masking tape). Explain that each child should put the handle end of a plastic spoon between his teeth and that you will place a piece of candy in the spoon of the first player in each line. Tell them that players should pass the candy to each other, spoon to spoon to spoon, without dropping it. If they drop the candy, the team should start again.

Power Charge

Review the Power Source verse. Ask children:

- Did you notice the verse says be patient with "everyone"? Have you ever been impatient with someone?

- How does it feel when someone is patient with you?

- How can you gain patience?

Alternate Voltage

Have children create skits relating two scenes: a situation that demands patience in which the person fails to be patient, and the same scene in which the person responds patiently.

CD-204072 • *180 Faith-Charged Games* • © Carson-Dellosa

Old-Time Movies

Starter

During the game, children will learn more about how the Commandments work in their daily lives.

Write the Ten Commandments on the board and read Exodus 20:20. Ask children:

- Can you think of rules that we must obey in our daily lives?
- What happens when drivers don't obey the rules of the road?
- What happens in our lives when we don't obey God's commandments?

Power Tools

- Copy of the Ten Commandments
- Old-fashioned clothing for children (to simulate the look of a silent movie)
- Cardboard tubes

Power Source

"Moses said to the people, 'Do not be afraid. God has come to test you, so that the fear of God will be with you to keep you from sinning.'"
Exodus 20:20

Silent Game

Explain to the children that they will be making a skit that is similar to a silent movie. If possible, show them a short old movie scene. Tell children in advance to dress in black and white clothing. (Boys could wear white shirts and bow ties and add fake moustaches. Girls could wear scarves in their hair.) Divide into teams. Have each team choose a director and a commandment to turn into a skit. When the teams are ready, have each team's director call for quiet on the set and announce, "Action!" Have teams take turns performing their skits. Explain that the audience will watch through cardboard tubes, passing their hands back and forth over the front of the tube to get the old movie flickering effect. After the skit, have the audience guess which Commandment they have seen. Remind them when making the skit to keep it funny, with exaggerated movements, funny facial expressions, etc.

Power Charge

Review the Power Source verse and the Ten Commandments. Explain that God's commandments should not be feared. They are His rules to help us win in the game of life. His guidelines keep us safe and happy. Ask children:

- How does obeying God's commandments keep us from sinning?
- What can we do to help us keep God's commandments?

Alternate Voltage

Have children memorize the Ten Commandments.

Polka-Dot Pizzas

Energy Level

Low

Starter

This crazy sentence-making game about food shows children that in the food world, certain ingredients do or do not go together. However, God put each of us together wonderfully, in His own image.

Read Psalm 139:14. Ask children:

- What does it mean when the Bible says that you are "fearfully and wonderfully" made?

Power Tools

- Copy of Mad Snack Sheet (see page 159)

Power Source

"I praise you because I am fearfully and wonderfully made; your works are wonderful, I know that full well." Psalm 139:14

Game-to-Go

Explain to the children they will be making a mad-snack creation. (Let them know that it is not edible.) Read the examples of the categories from the Mad Snack Sheet to get their creative juices flowing. Ask each child to name a description within a certain category. (For example, "Julio, name a kooky container"; "Trina, name a mad-jective." Write the children's answers in the blanks. When all of the blanks are completed, read the mad snack creation to the class. Play a few times to get even sillier results.

Power Charge

Review the Power Source verse. Ask children:

- Unlike our funny food combinations, God put good things together to make you. What are some of the special skills, talents, and dreams that He cooked into your personality?
- How could you use Psalm 139:14 to cheer up someone who does not like how God put them together?

Alternate Voltage

For more funny food fun, have children write and illustrate goofy menus of their favorite crazy food combinations.

Mad Snack Sheet

Kooky Containers

Barrels, a paper sack, a thimble, an ocean, dump trucks, a pocket, etc.

Mad-jectives

Polka-dot, smooshy, teeny-weeny, bubbly, watery, goopy, pink-striped, inflatable, neon, dinosaur-sized, oozing, melted, etc.

Cool Colors

Horse-hair brown, fat-caterpillar green, sunshiny yellow, tree-bark brown, dog-hair black, moldy orange, bubble-gum pink, etc.

Cooked-Up Crazy

Mustard-covered, flame-broiled, quick-frozen, freshly-painted, fork-tossed, quick-spun, freeze-dried, wet 'n' soggy, deep fried, crispy-corned, etc.

Fun Food

Cheeseburgers, mashed potatoes, apple sauce, pancakes, seaweed, rhubarb, orange juice, turnip greens, spaghetti, ice cream, etc.

Happy Topping

A 20-year-old sugar plum on top, slathered in sour whipped cream, sprinkled with butterfly sneezes, drizzled with pink chocolate, etc.

Mad Snack Creation

When _____ got home from church, he/she decided to make
        (kid's name)

him/herself a little snack. First, he/she needed something to put his/her snack in, so

he/she got out _____. In this _____, he/she put
     (kooky container)   (kooky container)

_____. "It's just not complete,"
(madd-jective)   (cool color)   (cooked-up crazy)   (fun food)

_____ said. So, he/she topped it with _____.
    (kid's name)   (happy topping)

Rap It Up

Starter

This game employs spontaneous rap-writing with rhymes and rhythms, while acknowledging God's greatness on a road trip.

Read Psalm 95:1. Ask children:

- What are some ways that we can worship the Lord?

- What is your favorite way to worship Him?

- Are there others places to worship God other than church?

Power Tools

- None

Power Source

"Come, let us sing for joy to the Lord; let us shout aloud to the Rock of our salvation." Psalm 95:1

Game-to-Go

Have children pat their legs, snap their fingers, "beat box," or make rhythm patterns by clapping their hands to provide the beat for a redeemed hip-hop style song that names their surroundings and praises the Lord. Have one child volunteer to be the lead vocal, and others may chime in with the filled-in-the-blanks portions (see underlined words below).

Here's a sample with the blanks filled in. For normal game play, children should fill in the blanks with things they see on the trip.

"We're driving down the road, havin' some fun, hey!
In the rain 'n' the clouds 'n' the light of the sun.
Lookin' out the window, 'n' what do I see?
Cars and tractors and buildings and gas stations and street signs and red lights,
Just rockin' down the road, happy as can be.
Drivin' along, and we never get bored, 'cause there's
Palm trees and blue skies and seagulls and bushes and dragonflies
And with all of these things we say, "Praise the Lord!"

Power Charge

Review the Power Source verse. Ask children:

- What do you do, when you know the Lord deserves your worship, but you don't feel like worshipping Him?

- Can you share a time when you felt closer to the Lord because you worshipped Him?

Alternate Voltage

Use percussion instruments for more rhythm.

Seek and Find, A to Z

Energy Level Low

Starter

One of the most simple, beautiful promises of the Bible is that if we seek God with our whole hearts, we will find Him! This game involves searching for things outside a vehicle, but it points to the greater adventure of searching for God with all of our hearts, and finding Him.

Read Deuteronomy 4:29. Ask children:

- Have you ever lost something important to you, and then looked for it very carefully until you found it?
- Were you looking for that item "with all your heart and with all your soul"?
- What does it mean to look for the Lord that way?

Power Tools

- Candy or snack items

Power Source

"But if from there you seek the Lord your God, you will find him if you look for him with all your heart and with all your soul." Deuteronomy 4:29

Game-to-Go

One by one, or in teams, have children name items they see that begin with a letter of the alphabet. Passengers on opposite sides of the vehicle can form teams. Each time they name five things for a particular letter, reward them with a piece of candy or a snack item.

Power Charge

Review the Power Source verse. Have a few children to put it into their own words. Ask children:

- Tell about a time when you were seeking the Lord and you found Him in a special way.
- What are some ways that we can seek the Lord?
- How can you seek the Lord this week?

Alternate Voltage

Incorporate a time limit for the game (for example, one minute per letter).

The Bible Is the Way-O

Energy Level

Low

Starter

For this game, the musical phrase from the children's song, "B-I-N-G-O" becomes, "B-I-B-L-E," and the fun takes flight into singing and a joy-filled love for God's Word.

Read Psalm 119:105. Ask children:

- Can you remember a time when it was dark, and you used a flashlight to find your way?
- How does God's Word act as a light to us spiritually?
- What makes the Bible such an important book in your life?

Power Tools

- None

Power Source

"Your word is a lamp to my feet and a light for my path." Psalm 119:105

Game-to-Go

Use the melody from the tune BINGO and change it to sing: "There is a boy (girl) who has a book, the Bible is its name-o. B-I-B-L-E, B-I-B-L-E, B-I-B-L-E. The Bible is its name-o!" After each chorus, ask a question about the Bible or from a recent lesson. When someone answers correctly, sing the song again. Change introduction lyric for fun.

Sample song lines:

What's the book with awesome stories?
What's that book that can change our lives?
What's the name of the book we love?

Power Charge

Review the Power Source verse. Ask children:

- Can you tell about a time when you had a question or needed to know what to do, and the Bible gave you the answer?
- When do you make time to read the Bible?
- If you don't already, make time every day to read God's Word. When would be the best time for you?

Alternate Voltage

Have children turn other classic children's tunes into Bible songs.

Now You See It

Energy Level
Low

Starter

The simplest objects can be the hardest to find, which encourages us as believers to ask the Lord to open our eyes to see Him in ways we may have missed Him before.

Read 2 Kings 6:8–23. Ask children:

• Why do you think the servant didn't see the spiritual army surrounding him?

• We know there are angels, God's armies, as well as the Devil's armies surrounding us, but we can't see them. What would life be like if we could see the spiritual world around us?

• How would you have felt if you suddenly saw the hills full of horses and chariots of fire?

Power Tools

• None

Power Source

"Elisha prayed, 'O Lord, open his eyes so he may see.' Then the Lord opened the servant's eyes, and he looked and saw the hills full of horses and chariots of fire all around Elisha." 2 Kings 6:17

Game-to-Go

Have children play a search game. Have each child take a turn being "it." Have her begin with the line, "I see something near or far, something here inside the car," or "I see something near or far, something there outside the car." Then, add just one clue: "and it's yellow," or "and it's made of rubber." Allow the searchers to guess three or four times before giving the answer. Allow more or fewer guesses as is age-appropriate.

Power Charge

Review the Power Source verse. Ask children:

• What do you think that servant thought when he saw the horses and chariots on the hills surrounding them?

• Tell about a time when you saw God at work in your life.

Alternate Voltage

For a challenge, have children play their search game by describing objects that are back at the church or classroom.

Loony License Plates

Energy Level Low

Starter

In this game, children observe license plates and try to "bring good," or at least find meaningful words, hidden in the letters.

Read Romans 8:28. Ask children:

- Put that verse into your own words. What does it mean to you?

Power Tools

- None

Power Source

"And we know that in all things God works for the good of those who love Him, who have been called according to His purpose." Romans 8:28

Game-to-Go

Have children observe license plates and based on the letters they see, try to make strings of words that make sense, either funny or biblical. Depending on their age, they may need help. It may take several nonsensical combinations before they get better. Do a few examples to get them started. For example: BFP = Big Funny Pig or GCP = God Changed Paul. Give extra points for Bible-related sentences.

Power Charge

Review the Power Source verse. Ask children:

- How does it make you feel, knowing that God is at work in your life and that He has designed all things to work for your good?
- As a Christian, you know that God has great purposes for you. What do you hope some of those purposes are?

Alternate Voltage

When your class returns to church, have the children create their clever Bible-related license plate ideas using cardstock and craft supplies.

Kooky Rhythms

Energy Level Medium

Starter

This clapping game is fun and reinforces one of David's worshipping Psalms.
Read Psalm 47:1. Ask children:

- When was the last time you clapped your hands?
- What would it sound like if an entire nation clapped their hands at once?
- Can we worship the Lord with our applause?

Power Tools

- None

Power Source

"Clap your hands, all you nations;
shout to God with cries of joy."
Psalm 47:1

Game-to-Go

Play this game with one clap-leader and one group, or two clap-leaders and two groups.
For two groups, divide each side of the bus into separate groups. Have the leader clap a
simple rhythm such as: CLAP, CLAP, CLAP-CLAP-CLAP. Explain that the group members
should echo that clap as accurately as possible. Practice this first simple clap rhythm a few
times, so that they get the idea that it should be repeated clearly—everybody clapping
in unison—for the game to work. (Until it becomes impossible for the group to repeat it
clearly, and that's when it gets funny.) The second clap rhythm should be a little bit longer,
or faster, and each one should build gradually, until, when the group tries to echo the clap
pattern, it turns into applause.

Power Charge

Review the Power Source verse. Ask children:

- How do you worship the Lord?
- Can you imagine clapping, or applauding, our Lord Jesus? How would that make you feel?
- What could you do the next time you worship, to really worship Him more truly and deeply
  than you ever have before?

Alternate Voltage

Select volunteers and have a Kooky Rhythms master challenge.

Wacky Stories

Starter

This funny way of connecting disconnected thoughts to make stories illustrates how enjoyable it is to use our talents, even if it's just for fun. But, the greater honor of using our talents brings glory to God and blessings to others.

Read Psalm 45:1. Ask children:

- What do you think, "My tongue is the pen of a skillful writer" means?

- Do you like to write? What do you like to write?

- What talents does God give us that we could use for His glory and to tell others about Him?

Power Tools

- None

Power Source

"My heart is stirred by a noble theme as I recite my verses for the king; my tongue is the pen of a skillful writer." Psalm 45:1

Game-to-Go

Explain that children will be writing a story together. Tell them that each child should contribute three to four words to a completely spontaneous story. In other words, she should make up the words on the spot, right after hearing the prior player's made-up words. The story should always start with "Once upon a time." It might begin like this:

Player 1: Once upon a time,

Player 2: A person was

Player 3: Talking to a

Player 4: Dinosaur, when a

The next player is always thrown for a loop, so the story gets funny really fast. To heighten the fun, limit the words to one or two per person. The story can also be more serious, such as retelling a Bible story, but this would more appropriate for older children.

Power Charge

Review the Power Source verse. Ask children:

- Have you ever been moved in your heart by a Bible verse?
- In what ways can we use our talents to bless the King of Kings?
- In what ways can we use our talents to bring laughter and joy to others?

Alternate Voltage

Introduce a concept before the story begins, such as friendship, patience, prayer, etc. Encourage children to incorporate the topic in the spontaneous story. This makes the game more challenging and cohesive.

The Silliest Symphony

Energy Level Medium

Starter

When children sit for long periods of time in a car, there's one thing that will almost always bring smiles to their faces: over-the-top silliness. And here it is, real silliness, complete with silly symphony, silly conductor, and hopefully lots of laughter, which is good for everybody.

Read Proverbs 17:22. Ask children:

- Have you ever felt like you had a "crushed spirit"? What happened?
- How and when did you start feeling better?
- What do you think this verse is saying to you?

Power Tools

- None

Power Source

"A cheerful heart is a good medicine, but a crushed spirit dries up the bones." Proverbs 17:22

Game-to-Go

Appoint an orchestra conductor, and explain that everybody else is an instrument—a silly instrument, of course. When the conductor points to a child, he makes a silly noise (pop, cowboy whoop, boing, bark, zoom, tweet, roar, etc.) for as long as the conductor points at him. Remind children that they should remember their sounds and be careful to obey the conductor. Once a child makes a sound, she should use it for the rest of that symphony. It can get funny when the conductor quickly moves from instrument to instrument.

Power Charge

Review the Power Source verse. Ask children:

- What things bring cheer to our hearts?
- Why do you think God invented laughter?
- Everybody seems to laugh a little bit differently. Why do you think God made people that way?
- How can you bring cheer to people who are feeling "crushed"?

Alternate Voltage

Encourage the conductor to wave his hands up or down to adjust the volume of the silly orchestra.

Who Wants to Be a "Spell-ionaire"?

Energy Level
Low

Starter

This Bible spelling bee game holds a secret mission. Colossians 3:23 invites us on a true adventure: turning our everyday tasks into expressions of love and service as we learn to do everything (even spell words) for the Lord's glory.

Read Colossians 3:23. Ask children:

- What kinds of things feel like work for you?
- What kinds of things are more like play for you?
- How do we do our work for the Lord?

Power Tools

- Simple instruments

Power Source

"Whatever you do, work at it with all your heart, as working for the Lord, not for men." Colossians 3:23

TV Show Game

Introduce the game by asking, "Can you spell *Zerubbabel*?" It's Bible spelling bee time, with easy words like *Adam*, medium words like *tithe*, and more difficult words like *Zerubbabel*. Have the children spell a variety of words, using the Bible as the spelling book. Fit the difficulty level to children's age and knowledge, but be sure to add a few challenges. To add some fun and whimsy, have simple instruments on hand: a stick and wooden block to tick off the seconds, a triangle for wrong answers, and a bell for the right answers.

Power Charge

Review the Power Source verse. Ask children:

- What does it mean to work at something "with all your heart"?
- What if you helped someone you really loved, like your mom or dad, or a special friend? Would it help you to do the chore more cheerfully?
- When we work for the Lord, can it change the way we work and how we feel when we're working?
- What's the next thing that you can do "for the Lord" and not just for yourself?

Alternate Voltage

Conclude the spelling bee with a lightning round, using rapid-fire words, with the better spellers.

Fruitful Living

Energy Level
Medium

Starter

This game gives children a chance to act up a little. Through the improvised skits, children can show how their responses would display the fruit of the Spirit.

Read Galatians 5:22–23. Ask children:

- What does it mean to "bear fruit" as a Christian?
- Which of the nine fruits is strongest in your life?

Power Tools

- 4 copies of Skit Starters (see page 170)

Power Source

"The fruit of the Spirit is love, joy, peace, patience, kindness, goodness, faithfulness, gentleness and self-control." Galatians 5:22–23

TV Show Game

Choose four children to be skit writers, four to be skit actors, and the rest to be the audience who should guess which fruit of the Spirit is on display. Children may switch roles for each skit, although some may choose not to be actors, and that's OK. Give each writer a copy of the Skit Starters to design the skit with an ending that displays that particular fruit of the Spirit.

Power Charge

Remind children that our lives should be about Jesus and showing His life as it shines through our lives. Ask children:

- Do you know someone who displays the fruit of the Spirit in her life?
- Which of the fruits of the Spirit is weakest in your own life?
- How can you strengthen that fruit?

Alternate Voltage

Bring in a variety of fruit for children to snack on while preparing their skits.

Skit Starters

LOVE

Gerald, the school bully, just walked onto the playground. Three Christians try to have a loving attitude as he cuts in front of them and grabs their playground toys.

JOY

Tricia wakes up with five new cowlicks, squirts toothpaste on her shirt, spills hot sauce on her jeans, and can't find any pencils. Now, she's late for school. How will she find joy?

PEACE

Walter needs peace and quiet to finish his homework in the library so that he can go to the ball game after school. But, the kindergarten Pots 'n' Pans 'n' Kazoos team is rehearsing there.

PATIENCE

It's Saturday morning, and Dori is ready to go to the zoo. But, her brothers keep delaying the departure by finishing oatmeal, getting dressed, hunting for shoes, etc.

KINDNESS

Brad Boysenberry is a famous author, stuck on himself, until he's trapped in an elevator with two of his greatest three-year-old fans and one "I could care less" teenager.

GOODNESS

Max and Janice won a million dollars. They have no children, so they leave for a shopping spree. They find two poor children on the steps of the first store.

FAITHFULNESS

Andrew and Caleb promised Mom they would clean their rooms, but they keep getting interrupted by text messages and phone calls.

GENTLENESS

Mr. Binkley hates gerbils. His two children have 100 gerbils! When they all escape, he must find them and take them gently to their cages.

SELF-CONTROL

Pierre Soufflé, a famous painter, is moving to a new house. Sloppy furniture movers are carrying his priceless paintings.

Tell the Truth

Energy Level Medium

Starter

Based on a classic TV game show, this game shows that eventually the truth prevails. It also encourages children to choose the way of truth.

Read Psalm 119:30. Discuss big choice we must make every day—to tell the truth. Ask children:

- Can you think of a time when you chose the way of truth?
- Why do some people lie much of the time?

Power Tools

- Index cards
- Table
- Three chairs
- Identical simple costumes for characters
- Tell the Truth questions (see page 191)

Power Source

"I have chosen the way of truth."
Psalm 119:30

TV Show Game

Create the question and answer cards for the players by copying the Tell the Truth information (see page 191) onto index cards. As the game show host, start by welcoming the audience. Then, welcome to the table Paul the Apostle #1, Paul the Apostle #2, and Paul the Apostle #3. They should be dressed in identical costumes. Provide them with answer cards to help them through the game. Explain to the audience members that they should ask the questions on their question cards (which you have given to them in advance), and that they will try to guess which one is the real Paul the Apostle. The game ends when you ask, "Will the real Paul the Apostle please stand?" The children will see if they chose the "true" Paul.

Power Charge

Explain that in the same way that the false Pauls were hiding in the costumes, we sometimes avoid the truth by hiding it, not telling the whole story, or pretending something never happened. Ask children:

- Can you a time you thought you hid the truth, but it came out anyway?
- Why does God ask us to choose the way of truth?
- Are you ready to make a commitment to be a more truthful person?

Scripture Survivors

Energy Level Medium

Starter

This game will remind children that God's Word will cause us to be more than survivors in any situation.

Read Psalm 119:105 and Romans 8:37. Ask children:

- Can you think of a time when you were actually in a dark place and a light helped you?
- Can you think of a time when God's Word helped you in a very important way?

Power Tools

- Coconut
- Banana
- 2 sheets of white poster board
- Tropical music CD
- CD player
- Challenges and the Promises text (see page 191)

Power Source

"Your word is a lamp to my feet and a light for my path." Psalm 119:105

"In all these things we are more than conquerors through him who loved us." Romans 8:37

TV Show Game

Prior to class, copy the Challenges and the Promises onto sheets of poster board and display them. Have children sit in a circle. As a class, read the promises and find each corresponding Scripture. Instruct the children to keep their Bibles open to each Scripture for rereading. Tell children to imagine that they are stranded on an island. Start the music and have children pass the coconut and banana around the circle. Explain that when the music stops, the coconut holder should pick a challenge. The banana holder picks a promise that should help the other player survive her tough time.

Power Charge

Review the Power Source verses. Ask children:

- Why is it so important to read God's Word every day and memorize it?
- What do you do during your regular Bible reading time?

Alternate Voltage

Darken the room and play the game by flashlight. (Remind children not to shine flashlights toward another person's face.) Afterward, serve tropical snacks such as pineapple and coconut crunch bars.

Lost in the Old Testament

Energy Level
Medium

Starter

In this game, children must listen to clues to identify the mystery Bible story from the Old Testament. Read Psalm 119:18. Ask children:

- Who can think of five exciting stories from the Old Testament?

- Who can name your favorite Old Testament story?

Power Tools

- Stopwatch

Power Source

"Open my eyes that I may see wonderful things in your law."
Psalm 119:18

TV Show Game

Divide into two teams. Announce the game with a dramatic voice, "Ladies and gentlemen, Trans-Dimensional Bus #195 suddenly took a wrong turn—SCREECH! CRASH!— and crash-landed in the Old Testament. I wanted to get off at 32nd Street, but now I'm lost in the Old Testament! I need someone to help me open my eyes so that I can see where I am! It should take the bus driver, Mr. Snickerton, two minutes to reset the broken time toggle, so you have two minutes to tell me where I am—starting NOW!"

Explain that children should ask questions to determine who and where you are. You are not a Bible character, just an unseen visitor who has landed in biblical times. Start the stopwatch. Is it day or night? What is the temperature? Are you inside or outside? Is it quiet or noisy? Who else is there?

Your secret location is the Old Testament Temple, at night, where a young boy (Samuel) sits up in bed and says, "Here I am." You don't know why he said that, since you didn't hear the voice of the Lord. You are lost in 1 Samuel, Chapter 3. When a team guesses correctly, look around as if your eyes have been opened and you are seeing things for the first time!

Power Charge

Read 1 Samuel 3:1–11 and read the story of the Lord calling to Samuel. Comment that our ears should "tingle" at the wonderful things God does in His Word. Ask children:

- God spoke to Samuel. How does He speak to us through His word?

- If you've drifted away from a daily Bible reading plan, what can you do to get back on track?

Alternate Voltage

To make the game simpler for younger children, select a Bible character to play. Allow them to ask you yes and no questions to determine who you are. Give initial hints if needed (for example, I am an Old Testament character).

Lost in the New Testament

Energy Level **Medium**

Starter

Children will enjoy identifying the mystery Bible story from the New Testament.

Read John 21:25. Ask children:

- Who can think of five exciting stories from the New Testament?
- Who can name their favorite New Testament Bible character?

Power Tools

- Stopwatch

Power Source

"Jesus did many other things as well. If every one of them were written down, I suppose that even the whole world would not have room for the books that would be written." John 21:25

TV Show Game

Divide into two teams. Announce the game with a dramatic voice, "I was riding my interstellar bicycle down to the corner coffee shop to get a double-frozen, extra latte, peppermint-pistachio, green tea cappuccino, with barbecue chips when it happened. The gears on my bike shot from 100th to 1,257th gear, and I skidded through time, landing with a clatter and a thud, lost in the New Testament! It will take me two minutes to set the gears to 100 and pedal home, so you have two minutes to tell me where in the New Testament I am—starting NOW!"

Explain that children should ask questions to determine who and where you are. You are not a Bible character, just an unseen visitor who has landed in biblical times. Start the stopwatch. Is it day or night? What is the temperature? Are you inside or outside? Is it quiet or noisy? Who else is there?

Your secret location is the New Testament, during the day, in the countryside, near a slope that drops toward the sea. Jesus has just cast demons into a herd of swine (pigs). They ran down the slope and splashed into the ocean. You are lost in Matthew, Chapter 8, Verses 28–34.

Power Charge

Read Matthew 8:28–34. Explain that when we read these wonderful stories, we want to make sure we know Jesus as our Lord and Savior. Ask children:

- God spoke to us through Jesus. How does Jesus speak to us through the Bible?

Alternate Voltage

For older children, allow them to write similar Bible mystery adventures to share.

Who Wants to Fill a Balloon with Air?

Energy Level
Medium

Starter

Similar to a suspense-driven quiz show, this game adds suspense and fun to a books-of-the-Bible quiz game.

Read Proverbs 4:5. Remind children that the better they know where the books are in the Bible, the better they will know the Bible. Ask children:

- Why do you think we should learn about the books of the Bible?

Power Tools

- Balloons
- Suspenseful music CD
- CD player
- 4 chairs
- Books of the Bible Sample Questions (see page 192)

Power Source

"Get wisdom, get understanding; do not forget my words or swerve from them." Proverbs 4:5

TV Show Game

Select four children to play each round. Have the first four players sit in chairs facing you, the host; give each player a balloon. Explain that each time a contestant answers a question correctly, he takes a big breath and blows into his balloon. When a contestant gives an incorrect answer, he has to let air out of his balloon. The first contestant to blow up his balloon wins. If a contestant is stumped, he can use one of his three "life-lines"—an opportunity to ask an audience member for help.

Power Charge

Review the Power Source verse. Ask children:

- What do you love about the Bible?
- Have you ever tried to read the Bible, and discovered parts that you didn't understand? What did you do to understand it better?
- Proverbs tells us to seek wisdom. How does reading the Bible help us receive wisdom?

Alternate Voltage

To increase the excitement, invite parents to join the audience or even sit in the players' chairs for a round.

The Verse Is Right!

Energy Level Low

Starter

There are different ways to hide God's Word in our hearts: hearing, reading, studying, memorizing, and having discussions about the Bible. In this Bible story guessing game, children will look at an illustration and guess the corresponding story and book of the Bible.

Read Psalm 119:11. Ask children:

- Why did God make the Bible a book of stories, rather than rules and commands only?

- How can we learn God's truth by reading Bible stories?

Power Tools

- 10–20 Bible story illustrations (with text or captions)

Power Source

"I have hidden your word in my heart that I might not sin against you." Psalm 119:11

TV Show Game

Collect several Bible story illustrations. Begin by showing the class an illustration without any preparation. Explain that the children should guess the corresponding story and book. Part of the decision can be based on the illustrations themselves. Be sure to have a few obvious ones like David and Goliath, as well as more difficult ones that depict stories with more generic imagery.

Power Charge

Select a few illustrations that depict children's favorite Bible stories. Ask children:
- What do you like about these stories?
- How can reading these stories help us live for God?

Alternate Voltage

Show clips from DVDs that depict Bible stories. Use the mute feature so that the children can only see the visuals as clues.

Bible Times Jeopardy®

Energy Level
Medium

Starter

Teams will enjoy playing this game and most importantly, gaining knowledge of God's Word—which always leads to wisdom.

Read 1 Chronicles 12:32. Ask children:

- How can we add wisdom to our lives?
- How can knowing God's Word help you as a young person and in your future?

Power Tools

- Coin for coin toss
- Buzzer: Each team should create their own unique buzzing sound or movement.
- Small prizes
- Bible Times Questions text (see page 192)

Power Source

". . . men of Issachar, who understood the times and knew what Israel should do."
1 Chronicles 12:32

TV Show Game

Explain to the children that they will follow a similar format to the TV version of the game. Divide into three teams. Have each team create a funny team name. Flip a coin to determine playing order. The starting team chooses a category. You read the "answer," and they should name the question to earn points. Start with the Bible Times Questions. Determine the point value for each question. Once you read the answer, give teams up to 10 seconds to confer among themselves. If they think they know the answer, they "buzz in." Then, they have another 10 seconds to provide the answer.

Power Charge

After everyone is settled, and just before prizes are awarded, ask children:

- Why should a person read God's Word every day?
- How would you help a friend who wants to start reading the Bible every day, but doesn't know where to start?

Alternate Voltage

Have a talented child learn the theme song from the TV show and play it during the game.

Are You Smarter than a Sunday School Teacher?

Energy Level
Low

Starter

Like the popular TV game show, the real goal for children playing this game is to eventually surpass even their teacher's knowledge so that they can be teachers themselves.

Read Psalm 119:99. Discuss how much fun it would be to actually be smarter than all of your teachers! Ask children:

- How do Sunday school teachers and pastors gain so much wisdom?
- Who do you admire as a person of great wisdom, love, and godliness?

Power Tools

- Bible
- Stopwatch
- Small prizes

Power Source

"I have more insight than all my teachers, for I meditate on your statutes." Psalm 119:99

TV Show Game

Using a Bible, allow children to take turns reciting a verse for you to find. Have them time you for 45 seconds, which should start when children say "Go!" Then, have children challenge you to a Bible verse find, using the same format as above. Reward students who beat your time.

Power Charge

Have children sit in small groups and discuss:

- What Bible story means the most to you?
- If you could be any character in the Bible, who would you be?

Alternate Voltage

Encourage children to challenge their family members to a Bible verse find.

Slime Time!

**Energy
Level**
Medium

Starter

This game takes relentless commitment, and so does taking time every day to seek the Lord in prayer and worship.

Read Psalm 27:8. Ask children:

- What does it mean to seek the Lord's face?
- Are you seeking the Lord's face?

Power Tools

- Bowl, one per child
- Enough lime gelatin to fill the bowls
- Several apples, sliced
- Towels and wipes for clean up
- Bibs or smocks

Power Source

"My heart says of you, 'Seek His face!' Your face, Lord, I will seek."
Psalm 27:8

TV Show Game

Explain to children that this version of bobbing for apples is extra fun and extra slimy. Have each child who is old enough to safely play take his turn dunking his mouth into a plastic bowl of lime gelatin. Remind children to keep their eyes closed and their mouths open, and grasp the apple slice in their teeth.

Power Charge

Break into small groups and discuss:

- This game took a big commitment! You had to get slimed and keep dunking your mouth until you found an apple slice with your teeth. In what ways does "seeking God's face" also take a big commitment?
- How can we seek God more deeply in prayer and in worship?
- What would happen this week if you made a commitment to have some quality "face time" with God every day?

Alternate Voltage

Substitute super cold water for a less messy, but wetter, version.

Run for the Prize

Starter

Ancient Greeks first introduced the Olympics. By New Testament times, the Olympic games were well-known. Early Christians may have watched various sporting events in the Colosseum in Rome. The apostle Paul said that we should live our Christian lives in the way that an athlete trains for an Olympic race. This game provides a good lesson in physical training.

Read 1 Corinthians 9:24–27. Ask children:

• How does an athlete train for Olympic races?

• Do they avoid distractions?

• What things can distract us from living a godly life?

Power Tools

• Prizes

• Items for obstacle courses, relays, and hurdles, such as boxes and chairs

• Stopwatch

• Masking tape

• Crepe paper

Power Source

"Do you not know that in a race all the runners run, but only one gets the prize? Run in such a way as to get the prize."
1 Corinthians 9:24

Ancient Tradition Game

Stage different types of races for the children to complete.

SPRINT: Have children line up at the starting line (marked with masking tape). Mark the finish line with crepe paper for the winner to break through. Give the signal and cheer the runners!

HURDLES: Place cardboard boxes about six to eight feet apart. Have children take turns running and jumping over the boxes to reach the finish line (marked with masking tape). Use a stopwatch to record finishing times.

RELAY RACE: Divide children into four teams; give each team a baton. Have each child run around a chair, return to her team, and then pass the baton to the next runner.

Power Charge

Have children assemble and award the prizes. Tell children that in our Christian lives everyone can get first prize by serving the Lord with all of her heart. Read 1 Corinthians 9:25. Ask children:

• Paul says that we go into "strict" training, much like an athlete. Name some parts of our strict training. (Reading the Bible every day, attending church, living like Jesus, memorizing Scripture, obeying God's commands, etc.)

• What is our crown that will last forever?

The Banquet's Last Drop

Energy Level
Low

Starter

In Bible times, just as now, there were many life events to celebrate: births, weddings, and religious holidays. In Bible times, food was served at banquets—large meals for friends and family. A banquet could last hours or even days. During a banquet, the guests found many ways to entertain themselves, such as singing, performing skits, or playing games. A game of skill called kottabos (KO-ta-bows) was played while sitting around the banquet table.

Read Luke 14:7–14. Ask children:

- How does your family celebrate special events? Who attends? What do you eat? Are there any traditional games that you play?

Power Tools

- Bull's-eye on a large, white piece of paper (adjust size as needed to increase level of difficulty)
- Water (or grape juice if spilling is not a concern)
- Plastic cups

Power Source

"When you give a banquet, invite the poor, the crippled, the lame, the blind, and you will be blessed." Luke 14:13–14

Ancient Tradition Game

The object of Kottabos was to flick the last drops of wine from one's cup as close to the bull's-eye as possible. Give each child a small plastic cup that contains a small amount of water. While holding the cup (and not letting it go), she should flick her wrist to expel the water toward the target.

Power Charge

In the Bible, Jesus told us not just to invite the people we like to a banquet. Instead, we should show hospitality to everyone, including those who are hard to love. Ask children:

- Are there children in your neighborhood, school, or sports teams that you could show unexpected hospitality to and invite to your next "banquet" (birthday party, sleep-over)?

Alternate Voltage

Play this game during snack time. Place a blanket on the ground for the table. You may place pillows around the blanket for seats. Explain that guests would lounge during meals in Bible times, instead of sitting in chairs.

Give Me the Next Word

Energy Level Low

Starter

Poems today are different from those of Bible times. Today, songs and poems are often written in rhyming sentences. Biblical poems and songs were often written with two lines that said similar things (called parallelism). Many famous people in the Bible wrote poems and songs this way, including Moses, David, and Solomon.

Read Deuteronomy 31:30. Ask children:

- What are some of your favorite poems?
- Have you ever written a poem?

Power Tools

- Proverbs Poetry (see page 192)

Power Source

"Moses recited the words of this song from beginning to end in the hearing of the whole assembly of Israel." Deuteronomy 31:30

Ancient Tradition Game

Read Deuteronomy 32:1–3. Ask children to listen for the similar words.

Listen, O heavens, and I will speak;
hear, O earth, the words of my mouth.   (listen/hear, speak/mouth)

Let my teaching fall like rain
and my words descend like dew,   (fall/descend, rain/dew)

like showers on new grass,
like abundant rain on tender plants.   (showers/rain, grass/plants)

I will proclaim the name of the Lord.
Oh, praise the greatness of our God!   (proclaim/praise, Lord/God)

Create a Proverbs Poetry worksheet and make a copy for each child. Have children fill in the missing words. (Answers: commands, heart, cry, treasure, God, wisdom, blameless, protects)

Power Charge

Biblical poems and songs were used to praise God and to share wisdom in Bible times. Ask children:

- Which types of poems do you like more? Why?

Alternate Voltage

Children may want to write their own poems using either rhyme or parallel lines to praise God. Younger children could write a class poem.

Via Dolorosa: Guess the Roman Rules

Energy Level

Low

Starter

This game board was found etched on a stone pavement along the Via Dolorosa (Way of the Cross). The Via Dolorosa is the path that Jesus walked from his trial before the Romans to the place where he was crucified in Jerusalem. When Jesus was crucified and rose again on the first Easter Sunday, the Romans were ruling most of Europe and the Middle East and had many soldiers stationed in the city of Jerusalem. The soldiers would play games while they were on duty to make time pass quickly. Scholars are not sure exactly how to play the game, but most believe it had a similar objective as checkers or backgammon.

Read Mark 15:21–24. Ask children:

- Have you ever created your own game?

Power Tools

- Game board (see page 192), one per four children
- Pennies or beads to use as game pieces
- Index cards, one per four children
- Dice
- Pens or pencils

Power Source

"And they crucified him. Dividing up his clothes, they cast lots to see what each would get." Mark 15:24

Ancient Game

Create a game board based on the design on page 192. The game board should be roughly 7" x 7" (17.8 cm x 17.8 cm). Divide into groups of four. Allow each group to examine the game board and invent rules for the game using game pieces. Begin by discussing the rules to common board games. Have each group write their game's directions on an index card. Allow time for children to play the games they have invented.

Power Charge

Review Mark 15:24. Ask children:
- How does it make you feel to think that soldiers could have played a game while Jesus was being crucified?

Alternate Voltage

Have children teach their rules to another group or to the class. Discuss the different variations that were created using the same board.

Scribal Scramble

Starter

In ancient times, a special group of people called scribes recorded events. (The "teachers of the law" mentioned in the Power Source verse were scribes.) A scribe's job was to accurately copy the material given to him. In New Testament times, the scribes not only copied texts, but they also interpreted it. Thus, when King Herod heard about a king being born in Bethlehem, he sought information from the priests and the scribes.

Read Matthew 2:1–6. Ask children:

• Would you like being a scribe? Why or why not?

Power Tools

• Alphabet Code (see page 190)

• Paper

• Pencils

• Chalkboard or white board

• Chalk or markers

Power Source

"When King Herod heard this he was disturbed, and all Jerusalem with him. When he had called together all the people's chief priests and teachers of the law, he asked them where the Christ was to be born." Matthew 2:3–4

Holiday Game

Write the Alphabet Code on the board. Have children write these numbers on their papers and then decode: 10, 5, 19, 21, 19, 23, 1, 19, 2, 15, 18, 14, 9, 14, 2, 5, 20, 8, 12, 5, 8, 5, 13. (Answer: Jesus was born in Bethlehem.) Have children create other Christmas messages for classmates to decode.

Power Charge

Encourage children to be grateful to God's Jewish people who have faithfully copied and protected God's Word through the centuries.

• What is one of your favorite Scripture verses or stories?

Alternate Voltage

Demonstrate how important exact communication is by playing the telephone game. Whisper the following sentence in the ear of one child. "Ezra was a scribe who copied texts in order to give them to a new generation." Have the children pass the message from one person to another until the last child tells you what he heard. Then, read the original sentence.

Heroes and Villains

Energy Level
Low

Starter

The book of Esther is the basis for the Jewish holiday of Purim (pew-REEM). The heroes are Esther and Mordecai. Mordecai saved the king's life by telling his cousin Esther (who was the queen) that people wanted to kill the king. Esther risked her own life by revealing this plot to the king. The twist in the story is that Haman, the king's prime minister, hated Mordecai. Haman even wanted to kill Mordecai and everyone who was related to him. At the end of the story, Haman is killed and Mordecai and his relatives are saved. The story is read each year during Purim.

Read Esther 6:1–11. Ask children:

• What are some qualities of a hero?

Power Tools

• Noisemakers (bells, drums, pencils on desk, clapping, etc.)

Power Source

"'What honor and recognition has Mordecai received for this?' the king asked. 'Nothing has been done for him,' his attendants answered."
Esther 6:3

Holiday Game

Hand out noisemakers and reread Esther 6:1–11. When this story is read, Jewish people cheer for Mordecai and should make noise at Haman. Instruct children that every time they hear Mordecai's name, they should cheer. When Haman's name is read they should make noises in order to drown out the sound of Haman's name.

Power Charge

Tell children that we should be careful when choosing heroes. Discuss what made Mordecai and Esther heroes. Mordecai refused to bow to Haman and told Esther about the plot to kill the king; Esther bravely approached the king to ask him to spare the lives of her Jewish people. It was God's plan to spare the Jewish people—His people—and Esther allowed God to use her for His purpose.

• Who do you consider to be a hero? Do heros always receive honor or recognition? Why?

Alternate Voltage

Have children list other heroes from the Bible, including reasons why they are heroes. Have them make a list of "villains" as well, including reasons why they aren't heroes.

Cleaning Out the Leaven

Starter

Passover is an important holiday in the Jewish calendar. It's the time to remember how God led the people of Israel from Egypt. During Passover, which lasts a week, there should not be any food items that contain leaven (yeast) in one's home. Leaven is usually found in breads. The Israelites were in such a hurry to leave Egypt that they did not have time to let their bread rise. Not eating anything with leaven is a reminder of the ancient Israelites' deliverance from Egypt. Observant Jewish families will spend days cleaning their homes and making sure that they have removed all of the leaven. This becomes a game in many homes, as the mother will hide one final piece of bread and let children search for it.

Read Exodus 12:1–20. Ask children:

- Are you responsible for any special holiday chores at your house?

Power Tools

- Bread
- Small plastic bags

Power Source

"For seven days you are to eat bread made without yeast. On the first day remove the yeast from your houses." Exodus 12:15

Holiday Game

Before class, hide slices of bread around the room. Give each child bags to collect the bread and then signal for them to begin searching. Award a prize to the child who finds the most bread. Remind children that they are looking for bread containing yeast. This should remind them of the Scripture passage.

Power Charge

After playing the game, review the definition of leaven (yeast, an item that makes bread rise). Yeast was used many times by Jesus in the Bible as a metaphor for sin. Read Matthew 16:11-12 and Galatians 5:9. Just a pinch of yeast in bread dough would affect the entire batch of dough. Jesus said that yeast was like sin, even a little bit could work its way through all areas of your life.

- How can we keep even a little bit of sin from penetrating all areas of our lives?

Alternate Voltage

Ask children to think of any other holiday celebrations that involve a fun search. If appropriate, play the game.

A Noisy New Year

Energy Level Low

Starter

Show children a calendar that includes the Jewish holidays. Have one child find the words Rosh Hashanah in either September or October. The words Rosh Hashanah mean "head of the year"—thus the Jewish New Year. Rosh Hashanah is also called the Feast of Trumpets. Trumpets are still blown on Rosh Hashanah. In fact, being well-practiced and able to blow the trumpet (called a "shofar" in Hebrew) in established patterns is considered a valuable skill.

Read Leviticus 23:23–25. Ask children:

- What is supposed to happen on the first day of the seventh month?

Power Tools

- Noisemakers (bells, drums, paper towel rolls for trumpets, etc.)

Power Source

"Say to the Israelites: 'On the first day of the seventh month you are to have a day of rest, a sacred assembly commemorated with trumpet blasts'." Leviticus 23:24

Holiday Game

Celebrate the Feast of Trumpets by having children blow their noisemakers in the same patterns that are used on Rosh Hashanah. Begin with a long blast (holding for nine beats or seconds); then, three short blasts (three beats each); then, nine very quick blasts in succession; and finally, a blast for as long as it can be held. Divide children into four groups and assign each group one of the sounds.

Power Charge

Discuss with children how traditions make holidays fun and interesting. Stress that with Rosh Hashanah, traditions go back thousands of years. Ask children:

- What events happen on January 1?
- Is there noise involved?
- Does your family consider it a sacred holiday?

Alternate Voltage

Have children compete for the best "trumpet player" on Rosh Hashanah.

You Shall Live in Booths

Energy Level Medium

Starter

Sukkot (sue-COAT), or the Feast of Booths, is a time to remember that God's people lived in tents when they wandered in the desert after the Exodus. Today, Jewish families observe this holiday by building and decorating booths, called sukkahs (sue-KAHs), where they enjoy meals, family time, and even sleep.

Read Leviticus 23:33–43. Ask children:

• Have you ever spent the night in a tent?

• Why were the Israelites required to live in booths?

Power Tools

• For the sukkah: a sun shelter, tent, or canopy can be used if you want all children to sit in it; however, a small sukkah could be built using draped sheets over a table

• Decorative items: garland, stringed lights, pictures, any decorations used for a Christmas tree

• Snack

Power Source

"Say to the Israelites: 'On the fifteenth day of the seventh month the Lord's Feast of Tabernacles begins, and it lasts for seven days.'" Leviticus 23:34

Holiday Game

Set up the sukkah before children arrive. Lead children to the sukkah. Explain that a proper sukkah should be tall enough for a man to stand in with three sides covered, and a roof that is not completely covered. (You should be able to see the stars.) Allow children to help decorate the sukkah. Explain that like a Christmas tree, each family has their own decorating style for their sukkah. Many families use lights, family pictures, and other items that make them rejoice in their heritage.

After decorating the sukkah, have children sit and read Exodus 15:1–19. Tell children that the Israelites sang this song after they saw God protect them and lead them from Egypt. Conclude with a snack and tell children that during this holiday, many Jewish people will eat all of their meals while sitting in the sukkah.

Power Charge

Review the Power Source verse. Ask children:

• What holiday celebrates Jesus' birth?

• What holiday celebrates Jesus' death and resurrection?

• What holiday celebrates God's provision during the Israelite's journey through the wilderness?

Spin the Dreidel

Starter

Hanukkah (HA-nah-kah) is an eight-day celebration also known as the Feast of Dedication. It occurs in either November or December. Hanukkah celebrates the victory of a small group of Jewish soldiers who reclaimed the Temple from enemy soldiers. When they searched for oil to light the menorah, a special oil lamp with several branches, they found only enough oil to last for one day. Miraculously, the lamp burned for eight days. Hanukkah celebrations often include storytelling, gift giving, special foods, and games such as Dreidel (a game using a four-sided spinning top). The Hebrew letters on the top stand for, "A great miracle happened there."

Read John 10:22–23. Inform children that Jesus celebrated Hanukkah. Ask children:

- What do you think about Hanukkah?

Power Tools

- A dreidel (can be found at stores before and during Hanukkah)
- Bag of small, individually wrapped candies (or pennies)

Power Source

"Then came the Feast of Dedication at Jerusalem. It was winter, and Jesus was in the Temple area walking in Solomon's Colonnade." John 10:22–23

Holiday Game

Give each child an equal amount of candy. Have children sit in a circle and select one piece of candy to begin. Explain that each child will take a turn spinning the dreidel. He has a few options: either do nothing, take all of the candy in the pot, take half of the candy in the pot, or give all of their candy to the pot, depending on which letter is faceup when the dreidel lands. Continue playing for as long as time permits or until one child has all of the candy. While children are playing the game, remind them what the letters mean and about the story behind the game.

Hebrew letter	Hebrew Word (translation)	Dreidel Action
Nun (נ)	Nes (miracle)	Do nothing
Gimel (ג)	Guh-dole (great)	Take all
Heh (ה)	Hi-yah (was)	Take half
Shin (ש)	Shom (there—rhymes with Tom)	Give all

Power Charge

Discuss how playing this game helps children remember the miracle. Ask children:

- What are some of your favorite holiday games?

Pages 23, 184

A	B	C	D	E	F	G	H	I	J	K	L	M	N	O	P	Q	R	S	T	U	V	W	X	Y	Z
1	2	3	4	5	6	7	8	9	10	11	12	13	14	15	16	17	18	19	20	21	22	23	24	25	26

Page 37

Possible Clues

- I like to sit in the back. (Under a chair in the last row)
- Picture, picture on the wall, who can hide the best of all? (Behind a picture)
- I love my 88 keys, and I'm never locked. (On the piano)
- He's in the lead, but he's not racing. (Pastor)
- Tap, tap, tap. Can you hear me now? (Under a microphone stand)

Page 53

- Matthew 16:16
- Mark 3:11
- Luke 22:70
- John 3:16
- Acts 9:20
- Romans 1:4
- Galatians 2:20
- Hebrews 4:14
- 1 John 4:15
- 1 John 5:5

Page 71

Our Father in heaven,	hallowed be your name,	your kingdom come,	your will be done	on earth as it is in heaven.
Give us today our daily bread.	Forgive us our debts,	as we also have forgiven our debtors.	And lead us not into temptation,	but deliver us from the evil one.

Page 72

- Stand on one foot.
- Turn around.
- Take a step forward.
- Do five jumping jacks.
- Twirl like a ballerina.
- Make a funny face.

Page 121

1. Good Shepherd .... John 10:1–18
2. Good Samaritan .... Luke 10:25–37
3. Growing Seed .... Mark 4:26–29
4. Lost Coin .... Luke 15:8–10
5. Lost Sheep .... Luke 15:4–7
6. Net of Fish .... Matthew 13:47–50
7. Prodigal Son .... Luke 15:11–32
8. The Sower .... Matthew 13:3–9
9. The Sheep and the Goats .... Matthew 25:31–46
10. Wise Builder .... Matthew 7:24–27

Page 128

Bible Questions

1. Name the first two people God created. *Adam and Eve*
2. Name the person who built an ark. *Noah*
3. Name the person who died for our sins. *Jesus*
4. Name the person who wrote the Gospel of Matthew. *Matthew*
5. Name the person who wrote the Book of Revelation. *John*
6. Name the person who baptized Jesus. *John the Baptist*
7. Name the person who said, "Let my people go." *Moses*
8. Name the person who denied he ever knew Jesus. *Peter*
9. Name the person who wrote the Book of Acts. *Luke*
10. Name the person who said, "I am coming quickly." *Jesus*
11. What is the first book in the Old Testament? *Genesis*
12. What Psalm says, "The Lord is my shepherd"? *Psalm 23*
13. What is the first book in the New Testament? *Gospel of Matthew*
14. What is your favorite Bible story? *Answers will vary.*
15. What happened when Noah finished the ark? *Rain fell for 40 days and nights, water burst from underground, and the earth flooded.*
16. How many tribes of Israel were there? *Twelve*
17. What is the second book in the Bible? *Exodus*
18. Name all four gospels. *Matthew, Mark, Luke and John*
19. What is the name of the last book in the Bible? *Revelation*
20. Which comes first, the New Testament or the Old Testament? *Old Testament*

Page 129

Bible Promise Reference List

1. Psalm 23:1
2. Joshua 1:9
3. John 3:16
4. Philippians 4:13
5. Ephesians 6:1-3
6. Philippians 4:19
7. Jeremiah 29:11
8. Nahum 1:7
9. Lamentations 3:25
10. Psalm 145:8
11. Luke 11:28
12. Matthew 5:19
13. Joshua 1:8
14. 1 John 2:10
15. John 6:35
16. Acts 2:28
17. Psalm 84:11
18. 2 Corinthians 9:8
19. Psalm 27:13
20. Matthew 6:33

Page 133

Sample Questions

Adam's wife was named _____. *Eve*
Adam and Eve lived in the Garden of _____. *Eden*
Baby Jesus was born in the city called _____. *Bethlehem*
Jesus' earthly father was named _____. *Joseph*
Jesus' cousin was named John the _____. *Baptist*
Noah built a big boat called the _____. *Ark*

The ark floated over the _____ _____. *Flood waters*
Moses met God at a burning _____. *Bush*
Moses was sent to talk to Egypt's leader, called _____. *Pharaoh*
Moses led God's people through the _____ _____. *Red Sea*

Page 171

Question Card 1: Have you written a lot of letters? **Answer Cards 1:** 1, 2, 3: Yes.

Question Card 2: Does your life involve dealing with churches? **Answer Cards 2:** 1, 2, 3: Yes.

Question Card 3: Have you ever changed your name, from a name you've used all of your life to another name? **Answer Cards 3:** 1, 2: Yes; 3 No.

Question Card 4: Were you chasing after Christians before your name changed? **Answer Cards 4:** 1, 2: Yes; 3 No.

Question Card 5: Are you a person who has given his life to knowing the Scriptures? **Answer Cards 5:** 1, 2, 3: Yes.

The real Paul the Apostle is **Paul #2**.

Paul #1 studied the Scriptures in school, but when a teacher gave him a B- in Ark Building 101, he got mad at all religious people. He even changed his name from Mordecai to Frankie. Later, he repented and used his skills as a woodworker to help Christians build houses for church meetings. To contact people who wanted to build church-type houses, he had to write a lot of letters.

Paul #3 worked as a Scripture copier in New Testament times, so he wrote a lot of letters and learned the Scriptures at the same time. He would copy the writing onto papers called scrolls, and then deliver them to the Temple. He actually considered changing his name, from Mephistocletees to Tim, but he would have had to go back and change all of the scrolls where he had signed the last page (in tiny letters) "Copied by Mephistocletees."

Page 172

The Promises correspond with the Challenges, in order.
Challenges

- You seem to be alone on the island, and you hear strange noises.
- You're waiting for a helicopter to come for you, and you're bored.
- You're trying to fix a suspension bridge, but it's difficult.
- You know God called you here, but you're beginning to wonder if He really will see you through.
- You've been praying for a good friend on the island, but it hasn't happened yet.
- When you look at the night stars, God seems so far away.
Promises

- Do not fear: Genesis 15:1 and Deuteronomy 3:22
- Praise: Exodus 15:2
- Strength: Psalm 31:24
- Trust: Psalm 13:5
- God will answer: Psalm 50:15
- God is near: James 4:8

Page 175

Books of the Bible Questions

- Name the first book of the Bible. *Genesis*
- Name the last book of the Bible. *Revelation*
- How many Gospels are there? *Four*
- How many Old Testament Gospels are there? (trick question) *None*
- How many Psalms are there? *150*
- What are the names of the Gospels? *Matthew, Mark, Luke, John*
- Name the first five books of the Old Testament. *Genesis, Exodus, Leviticus, Numbers, Deuteronomy*
- Name the Major Prophetic books. *Isaiah, Jeremiah, Lamentation, Ezekiel, Daniel*
- How many Corinthian letters are there? *Answers will vary.*
- Who wrote the Book of Jude? *Jude*
- How many Bible books did John write? *Five*

Page 177

Answers and Questions

Bible Foods

Manna: *What food did God's people eat in the wilderness?*

Five loaves and two fish: *What food did Jesus multiply to feed the five thousand?*

Broken bread and wine: *What did the disciples eat with Jesus at the Last Supper?*

Bible Names

Noah: *Who built the ark?*

Moses: *Who led God's people from Egypt?*

Paul and Silas: *Which two followers of Jesus sang hymns in jail?*

Bible Creatures and Animals

Snake: *What animal tempted Adam and Eve in the Garden of Eden?*

Donkey: *What animal did Jesus ride into Jerusalem?*

One sheep out of 100: *What animal was missing in Jesus' story of the Good Shepherd?*

Page 182

Proverbs Poetry

> **Proverbs Poetry**
>
> **Proverbs 2:1**
> My son, if you accept my words
> and store up my _____ within you,
>
> **Proverbs 2:2**
> turning your ear to wisdom
> and applying your _____ to understanding,
>
> **Proverbs 2:3**
> and if you call out for insight
> and _____ aloud for understanding,
>
> **Proverbs 2:4**
> and if you look for it as for silver
> and search for it as for hidden _____,
>
> **Proverbs 2:5**
> then you will understand the fear of the LORD
> and find the knowledge of _____.
>
> **Proverbs 2:6**
> For the LORD gives _____,
> and from his mouth comes knowledge and understanding.
>
> **Proverbs 2:7**
> He holds victory in store for the upright,
> He is a shield to those whose walk is _____,
>
> **Proverbs 2:8**
> for He guards the course of the just
> and _____ the way of His faithful ones.

Page 183

Via Dolorosa

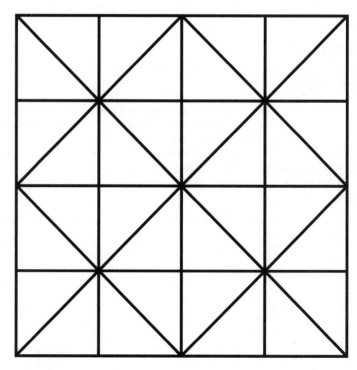